Diana McSweeney 12/2012

W9-AYZ-787

The Belt

The Belt

A NOVEL BY

Ahmed Abodehman

TRANSLATED FROM THE FRENCH BY
Nadia Benabid

Ruminator Books
SAINT PAUL, MINNESOTA

A copublication of

Ruminator Books   Saqi Books
1648 Grand Avenue   26 Westbourne Grove
St. Paul, MN 55105 (USA)   London W2 5RH (UK)
www.ruminator.com   www.saqibooks.com

First Ruminator Books/Saqi Books printing 2002

Originally published as *La Ceinture,* copyright 2000
Éditions Gallimard, Paris

Book design by Wendy Holdman
Typesetting by Stanton Publication Services, St. Paul, Minnesota

Printed in the United Kingdom

10 9 8 7 6 5 4 3 2 1

British Library Cataloguing-in-Publication Data

The right of Ahmed Abodehman to be identified as the author of this
work has been asserted by him in accordance with the Copyright,
Designs and Patents Act of 1988.

ISBN 0 86356 307 4

A catalogue record for this book is available from the British Library.

Library of Congress Cataloging-in-Publication Data

Abodehman, Ahmed.
    [Ceinture. French]
    The belt / by Ahmed Abodehman ; translated by Nadia Benabid.
        p.   cm.
    ISBN 1-886913-55-2
    1. Abodehman, Ahmed. 2. Assir (Saudi Arabia)—Social life and
customs. I. Benabid, Nadia. II. Title.
    DS247.9.A83 A3 2002
    953.8—dc21

                                2002005127

To my Arabia,
and to all the villages of the world

Contents

Prologue

My name is Ahmed ben Saad ben Mohammed ben Mouid ben Zafir ben Sultan ben Oad ben Mohammed ben Massaed ben Matar ben Chain ben Khalaf ben Yaala ben Homaid ben Chaghb ben Bichr ben Harb ben Djanb ben Saad ben Kahtan ben Amir. I probably should have stopped at Kahtan, like all Kahtanis who claim to belong to the most noble tribe in Arabia, and in all probability the wellspring of all things Arab. Some Kahtanis, however, often add the Amir to include the original ancestor, the Adam of the tribe, so to speak, and I am doing likewise because I'd much rather be a descendant of Adam than a descendant of Kahtan!

I am one of those rare Saudis who can still rattle off their genealogies by heart; I memorized it for my circumcision, it so happens. Germaine Tillon writes in her book *Le Harem et les Cousins* that the practice of circumcision in Arabia predates the Prophet by a thousand years. What this means in essence is that I was circumcised as boys had been in my tribe for 2,500 years. My childhood and youth, in other words, hark back to a kind of prehistoric time. I am a historical vestige, if you like. Not too long ago, I decided to visit a pedicurist. It was a first for me—and for him, too, I imagine because he spent hours removing the callus from the soles of my feet, even finding small pieces of thorn embedded in them, like fossils in limestone.

But here I am among all of you, in Paris at the dawn of the year 2000. Imagine the adventure of it for someone who couldn't even tell you his exact date of birth! You probably haven't noticed me because I make an effort to be like you, when in fact I carry the inexhaustible fire of my village inside me. At first, in Paris, I used to say hello to everybody, even in the subway, and even after I realized I was being completely ignored, I kept on greeting people, but in a murmur so faint only I could hear it. I wanted to share everything, like the time I took the train to Besançon. I had purchased a ham sandwich, mistaking it for a pastry. I asked the man sharing my compartment if he wanted a piece of my "cake." He wanted to know if I was a Muslim. I told him I was, and he explained that my snack was really bread with pork and continued to bolt down his mouthwatering dates without once pausing to offer me any.

When I finished my schooling in Riyadh, I was given the option to attend university in the United States, Great Britain, Germany, Spain, or France. I chose the land of Éluard and Aragon and Prévert. All in all, this explains why I gave voice to my village in French and how I came to be the first from all the countries of the Arabian Peninsula to write in this language, a fact I am sure some French readers will find to their taste and some Arab ones will not.

Writing, for me, is both a way of sharing and reinventing the world. I had to come to Paris to behold my country and my village; at home, I had simply been a poet. In Paris, I became a man in my own right, which is the true meaning of modernity. Whereas my tribe, even today, sees me as nothing more than a small cell in its great body, and a black cell at that for those members of the tribe who take a dim view of my marriage to a foreigner, a Frenchwoman as it happens. I understand them, and I am writing to tell them that there are others who understand me, understand us even better than we understand ourselves.

The Belt

His Wife's Wife

"Keep our secrets, dear God, and those of our kin, forever sealed!" This was the prayer the villagers uttered day in, day out, morning, noon, and night. All except for the wise Hizam, who was himself the biggest secret yet and the true mystery in the village. Like everybody, he too would raise his head toward the sky, but wordlessly—his mouth, it was no secret, crammed with the raisins and dates he was always munching on.

On seeing me one day join the others in prayer, he swept up a handful of sand and pelted me in the face. I didn't even wince; it was common knowledge in the village that Hizam was never wrong. "You shouldn't be praying with the rest of them," he said. "They're transient souls, people who take life one day at a time and never trouble themselves about the village, about really knowing it. This prayer is a pact of sorts, a pledge to live every new day to the fullest, leaving some mark upon the earth, even if it's something as fleeting as embracing a tree. That was the way of our forefathers, the way they built this village. Every stone, every leaf, every water well, every poem, every footfall filled with the breath of life, with love, hope, and suffering, with the achievements and disappointments of men who woke up each morning and sang the praises of their village as if it had only one day left to live. Those days are long gone, alas, and I'm the last man standing who can still answer for the soul of this village. And before you know it, I too will die, and then it'll be up to you, there's no one else."

Hizam didn't leave me much choice. Nor did he waste any time before putting me to the test by asking me to reach high up and touch the sky, to stir up a storm with my eyes, to turn myself into a stone. He asked about the things I had seen and felt and learned upon coming into this world: had I known from the start if I was a girl or a boy? I reached up and grazed the sky and brewed up a storm in my head and turned myself into a stone, and, for the first time ever, wanted to be a cloud. To pull me out of my addled state, Hizam asked to see my knife.

"You'll see it when the time comes."

"The time has come. Let me see it and I'll tell you if you're a boy or a girl."

"By my knife?"

"Of course, by your knife. What is a man if not a knife? Everything about a man, his words, his eyes, his actions, even the way he sleeps, is like a knife. A man's knife is his conscience. Look at women, if you don't believe me, always carrying on as if they were beyond reproach."

Hizam placed the blade against his skin and tried shaving his leg without much success. And when he sent it sailing toward a rock, the steel chipped. I stood by, humiliated and crushed. I couldn't help feeling his disappointment. Still, he did all he could to console me.

"God made the male like a knife, able to cut all things at all times. The knife makes the man, not the beard or the genitals."

"I'll be that knife you dream of, Hizam, I promise."

Hizam knew me well. He knew, for example, that all I had to do was look at people to see inside their souls; I could see it all and could never, never keep any of it to myself. It really didn't matter much if the secrets were mine or someone else's. Sooner or later, and despite my every good intention, they were bound to become public knowledge. I would tell relatives and friends and even people I met in passing, and in exchange, they invariably divulged some extremely intimate and private thing about themselves. Maybe they did it because I had no secrets of my own. Hizam, who increasingly referred to me as the Scandal, admitted one day that his daily intake of figs and raisins had greatly increased ever since I had taken it into my head to start talking. I did, however, have one secret, dear to me as life itself, and I've only told that one to a photograph of my father.

Once, in a daydream, I saw the villagers wake up one morning to find a meticulous record of their deeds, precise to the last detail, that I had posted on the door of our house the previous evening. They were falling all over one another, crying and kissing. In the evening, the village head called us to his house, and there we were, men, women, and children all gathered in one place for the first time. He sang and danced and smiled and grinned and showed us all his teeth. He didn't behave like a village head at all, and to clear up any lingering doubts, he resigned on the spot from all his duties. A village without secrets, he explained, did not need a village head. Everyone was all smiles the next day. Never have you seen such smiling. Life became a poem, people spoke to one another in verse, even in the dead of night, people were singing and composing poems. Lamps burned in every home, right through to sunrise sometimes. In this dream, I no longer was the village poet, the one and only, and the village no longer had anything to hide.

At home, we were four: Mother, whom I adored, Father, whom I loved, My-Sister-My-Memory, and me, the poet. Mother taught me poems and Father taught Sister songs. One couldn't have wished for a more ideal family!

I didn't like cities. Cities, Father once told me, had been invented by merchants and politicians for the benefit of merchants and politicians, and it took a true familiarity with the contents of a lady's handbag to really understand them. Father also used to say that it's, far better to see a woman than to look at her. Mother was the only woman I had ever really seen. And I more than loved her, I adored her. The one time I lied to her, she told me she had eyes and ears, hands and noses everywhere, even inside me. I never tried again. Once, when she made me angry, I walked away from her and cursed her in my head. She stopped me in my tracks, wanting to know why I was maligning her father, and naturally, she wasn't mistaken. She could read my mind, my most intimate thoughts. "Only a mother can open all doors," Father used to say. Her smell, her eyes, her beauty were food to my soul. And there wasn't a single person in the village who wouldn't have recognized her by that smell alone, as fragrant and unmistakable as the one of the bread she baked daily.

Cleanliness was the cardinal rule in our house. Mother, who was always making a great to-do about it, never once managed to have Father eat without splattering his clothes. Mealtimes for Sister and me, with Father doing his fair share, were always an excuse for fun and mischief. At such times, it felt like we were all three of us Mother's children. One day, a woman from the village hailed Father with insults. "You are nothing but your wife's wife!" she said. I heard her and was appalled, so chagrined I had to ask him if he had a pecker. Father, who had never once lied to me in his life, looked away and said no. I spent the next days wondering if I indeed had a father or two mothers.

I was haunted by a story I heard once. It happened in my mother's village. One day, a recently widowed man wandered into the village carrying his infant daughter, who couldn't have been more than a few days old. The villagers offered him food and shelter, and a number of women came forth and volunteered to nurse the child. But the man had taken a vow, and he had closed his wife's eyes with a promise to raise their child single-handedly and never to set foot in another house as his only home was the one he had shared with her and now it, too, was gone. The man rarely ventured from the mosque and spent all his time there, clutching his daughter to his side, never allowing her out of his sight. At first, anyone who listened could hear the child crying at night. Later, the crying subsided and before long, people began to notice the baby thriving. And that's when we all learned how love and necessity could turn a father into a mother.

The woman who had insulted Father was always finding ways to scoff at paternity as an inexact science. Every night, Father came back dead tired and Sister and I would minister to him by rubbing his feet and massaging his back and legs. I was always petrified at the thought of what I might uncover, dreading all possibilities equally. As we were leaving the mosque after Friday prayer one day, the village head called all the men to the great tree that graced the village square and announced that a penis had been mislaid. Every man there did a quick check of his underbelly and as nothing seemed amiss, the crowd soon disbanded. Only Father and I stayed behind and followed the village head, who seemed to have cinched the matter of the missing penis, back to his house. He invited us inside and kept us for lunch. We chatted about this and that while we ate. When the time came for us to leave, he reached into his pocket and produced a large and instantly recognizable key and handed it over to Father, who immediately fastened it to the belt that girded his hips. It was a village custom for the man of the house to be the keeper of the key to a room that was off limits to everyone else and where special provisions intended for guests and visitors were stored. This was to ensure that he would always have enough flour, butter, coffee, sugar, honey, and cardamom on hand for his guests and would never be caught short in the event his wife had run out of supplies. Any man who handed the key to this room over to his wife was, by definition, his wife's wife.

"To each plant its own sweet rain," Father used to say, and "it's far better to be a tree than a man come spring."

He would strip down to almost nothing and stand in the spring rain, urging me to join in. We were right in the middle of irrigating a field one time, and Father stopped what he was doing for the call to prayer. He had a beautiful voice, especially when he was addressing God. Plants, trees, rocks, even mountains seemed to listen when he called. I hurried, as I always did, because I, too, wanted to pray with him and because it's far preferable to pray in the company of others. But that day, Father said he wanted to be alone. I wondered why he was punishing me. He crouched behind a wall, and I noticed how threadbare his *thob* had become, the fabric ragged from years of wear, barely holding together where it rubbed up against the leather belt. I had never before seen my father naked, and at long last, I could breathe a sigh of relief. Later, I stood by his side and prayed as I had never prayed before.

Shortly before sunset and the first of the evening prayers, the men would gather in the village square. This was when news from neighboring villages would be shared and stories exchanged about the conflicts and disputes that were piling up before the judge the government had recently assigned to the region. One evening, as everyone milled about, waiting for the evening call to prayer, a woman appeared and made a beeline for the congregated men—I watched and gaped because no one had ever seen anything of the kind in our village. A heavy silence trailed behind her, and then the men made a quick dash for the mosque. I waited until after prayers to ask Father about the extraordinary thing we had witnessed. He ignored my questions. But as soon as we set foot inside the house, Mother was ready for him. "Well," she said by way of greeting, "you'll have to bite your wicked tongues now. Poor woman had to show blood from her own gut to keep the lot of you satisfied!" Father lowered his eyes and said nothing. Sister, on whom my bafflement was not lost, called me out to the roof terrace, where she explained that the woman was a widow who was rumored to be expecting a child. To put an end to all the talk, she picked a time when she knew the "monsters" (this is how women refer to men when these things come to pass) would all be gathered in one place to walk into their midst wearing a blood-soaked cloth, parading her menstrual blood for all to see. Sister and I came back into the sitting room. Mother was almost done lecturing Father, and in conclusion she told him, and by extension all the other village monsters, "You can now all rest assured that woman has become a man." For the sake of all married women, widows had to essentially become men in order to protect their person and the holdings that had been bestowed on them by their departed husbands.

The Little Prophet

The holy month of Ramadan was drawing near and the village had already picked out the ten boys, all about fifteen years of age, who were to be circumcised. For us circumcision is the ultimate test of strength and courage. It enacts the will of the father, and above all else, of the maternal uncle. "The maternal uncle is in the depths of the vagina," says the proverb. There, where he can fashion a nephew. My own uncle taught me those words. He loved me, and Mother used to say he was my second father.

Circumcision was a matter for the entire village, for the tribe as a whole. All the designated boys became brothers for this event and their mothers, mothers to all the boys. Our neighbor Sharifa, for example, was Mother Sharifa to me, whereas my real mother was simply Mother. The same applied to fathers, and the custom lives on to this day. One of my many mothers never tired of saying how she wished I would always remain little so that she could kiss my mouth forever. But the age of circumcision was bearing down on me, alas.

AHMED ABODEHMAN

But this time around, it was the turn of the older
boys, and on the feast day that marks the end of Ramadan, they were circumcised. Each boy was expected to
recite a long poem extolling the bravery and nobility of
his forebears and honoring all paternal and maternal
ancestors and to raise a pair of heavy, flashing daggers
high into the air and clash them repeatedly for the du-
ration of the ceremony, with every maternal uncle and
everyone in the village looking on.

The first boy stepped forward; someone had dressed
his hair with butter and crowned his head with a
wreath of mountain flowers, and launched into his
poem. The daggers he raised in his hands shone in the
sun. Our village boasted one of the most renowned circumcision masters. Word of his speed and skill had
spread throughout the region. The crowd parted to
make way for him when he arrived. In keeping with
custom, the boy never allowed his eyes to meet the
Master's and fixed his stare on the daggers and, without
once faltering, recited the long poem that enumerated
his genealogy. By now, the place was ablaze with the
screams of the women. The Master tucked the boy's
clothing up around his belt and began cutting into the
flesh of his genitals. Blood sprayed down the boy's legs,
puddling everywhere on the ground beneath him, but
the boy never once interrupted his recitation or allowed
his daggers to slump or showed a single sign of weakness. You would have thought the Master was slicing

14

into stone. The slightest hint of frailty, even one garbled word, could spell social death, and what village girl would be proud to call herself his wife after that?

Several days after the ceremony, one could still see trails of blood weaving their way out of the village square to the doorways of homes where circumcised boys were recovering. Special powders milled from various rocks and the sap of fig tree leaves were the traditional balm for these glorious wounds, and the boys were treated to copious morning meals of brown bread, sizzling butter, and mountain honey. Every morning, the boys would loll about naked in the sun to speed their healing. And for those appointed hours, everyone in the village respected their privacy.

When it was my family's turn to host the boys to breakfast, Mother sent me out to intercept them and keep an eye out for any girl who might stray into their vicinity. One of my cousins, however, a wild and perfumed beauty with a body whose sensuousness was all the more accentuated by the tightness with which she fastened her belt, somehow managed to elude my watchful eye. With ten meters or so between her and the boys, she addressed the handsomest one among them and promised she would make *todraa* with him after his full recovery. She was referring to the village custom that allowed all circumcised boys to make love in the village style, which meant leaving the boy unsupervised with a girl to exchange caresses, on the condition they both remain fully clothed and promise to go no further.

My cousin, it seemed, had no intention of giving the unfortunate boy she had set her sights on a chance to heal. Very slowly, she began to raise her skirts, and, with a flash of her thighs, she assured him of her readiness to "go all the way." Her little game was more than all those poor boys with their fresh wounds could bear. Blood began to flow anew, and their howling filled the street. As it happened to be a market day, the village was emptied of men, and the women, who were not allowed to come near the boys, looked on helplessly. Eventually, after the boys had cried their hearts out, some of the older women helped them refasten their bandages.

My cousin, as she got older, was spurred to greater and greater acts of provocation … but that's something about which I cannot say much. The village also has its silences.

The woman who wished I would always remain little so that she could kiss my mouth forever was among the first in the village to own a radio. Night after night, we would go to her house to listen to a program of Bedouin songs. From time to time, Father came with us, but more often than not, he didn't. Maybe because he didn't want to fuel idle gossip.

This woman lived with her children and kept two young women with her as companions. Both were beautiful and neither was shy about taking me in her arms, even in full view of the woman who wished to kiss me all her life. Sister never tired of saying what a handsome boy I was. And the girls in a neighboring village nicknamed me the Little Prophet.

I've already told you about Sister, but actually, I had six sisters at the time: three whom my father had been left by his brother and that brother's wife, who, as it happened, was my father's sister-in-law twice over, because in addition to being his brother's wife, she was also the sister of my father's first wife. As for Mother, she also was married once before to a very rich man from the neighboring village where all the girls knew me as the Little Prophet. Mother gave birth to ten children with that man. Six died, leaving me with two sisters and two brothers on my mother's side. This meant I had two sisters by my mother as well as three more who had been born to my mother's niece, because the wife of my paternal uncle was also the daughter of my maternal uncle.

My mother's first husband, though rich, had repudiated her on the spot for stealing a handful of coffee beans and giving them to a poor family who had gone without for weeks. The judge granted her guardianship of her youngest child, and, with the girl in tow, Mother sought refuge in her brother's home—that is to say with one of her many brothers, for she, too, had one half brother and three half sisters on her mother's side, and two half brothers and one half sister on her father's side. In a very short span of time, Father had lost not only his brother and sister-in-law, but also his first wife, who died in childbirth together with a newborn son. Father thus became the father to his brother's three daughters.

When he was a young man, Father was a Prince of the Night. He'd cover long stretches on foot to take part in festivities and nights of dancing. His music and mastery of the dance drove others to unrestrained delirium. People called him *raadane*, the lightning rod, bringer of storms. He wore his hair long, the nap so thick he once burned his scalp with the hot iron poker he used to trace the part that ran from the top of his brow to the base of his skull.

So Mother had gone back to live with her brother who was both my father's father-in-law and the grandfather of the three cousins who were soon to be my sisters. As luck would have it, my maternal uncle took in not only my mother but my recently widowed father as well. As village head, his door was open to all comers and his goodness plain on the wide and open face that was as vast as heaven and earth together. And as village heads go, there was none better. Father was always saying what pride and joy it gave him to know I was the nephew of such a great man.

Uncle believed that if there was any woman who could make a man out of the Prince of the Night, it was

Mother. But it took some doing to convince Father. Everyone knew that the second marriages of repudiated women tended to be short-lived, with the woman doing everything in her power to make life a living hell and driving her new husband to despair so he'd end up divorcing her and opening the way for her to go back to her ex-husband and the children she had been made to leave behind. Father, who was wise to the usual sequence of events and poor and a night owl to boot, had every reason to be suspicious of Mother's true intentions, especially as she made no secret of her longing for the children she had borne the wealthy man.

In the end, they married, a deed I'm always ready to pat myself on the back for, and my maternal uncle went from being my father's father-in-law to becoming his brother-in-law. Mother took her small daughter, my half sister, and moved into the empty house that had nothing to show for itself except for its occupants— Father and his three nieces, my future sister-cousins. Mother's first husband had remarried in the meantime. Only one daughter was born of this union, and in no time at all, he repudiated his new wife and married twice over in a matter of months. This was his way of punishing Mother, his one and only pearl among women, as he told me one day.

Mother did everything in her power to ensure the success of her marriage to Father, and I've always known I was her greatest pride and joy. Her first husband claimed she made me to get even with him. His own daughter grew up to be not only one of the greatest beauties but also one of the bravest women we had ever seen in those parts. She fell in love with a married man all the girls dreamed of marrying, and she managed to bring her wealthy and all-powerful father around to blessing the union. Never before had anyone pulled off anything of the kind. My half brothers and half sisters later told us how she took the old man on: "Regardless of your wishes," she said, "he is the one I'll marry. One of these afternoons, I'll just walk away from the herd, I'll leave the goats and sheep to fend for themselves and go straight to his house in broad daylight and in plain sight." Today, she is one of the happiest women on earth; she lives with her ten children in a house she shares with her husband's first wife and that woman's ten children.

My parents could count on Uncle to help with food and shelter, but there never seemed to be enough wood to keep the cooking fires going. Mother was not exactly a stranger to these parts. Many women from her village had married into my father's village, including one of her sisters, who later gave birth to that wild beauty who whetted the passions of men and with whose mischief you're already familiar.

To my knowledge, ours is the only tribe that was engendered by the sky. The place where we live is mountainous, and the sky is part and parcel of these mountains. Rain, here, does not fall, it ascends. Mother had to go into these mountains to forage for the dry wood that was essential for our daily sustenance.

She had been married two days when she set out for the first time with other women from the village. They left in the middle of the night. They had to be back by first light to lend a hand in the fields and tend to the children and animals. As they made their way home with the wood bundled onto their backs, they broke off for their morning meal. All the women took out loaves of bread, all except for my mother, who, under cover of darkness, chewed on the rope with which she had fastened the wood to her back. There was no bread to spare at her house. The other women, who suspected as much, pressed her to share their meager meals, but she just stood there quietly and chewed on her rope. Her companions never did figure out what she was eating because she was at the head of their small procession with her back turned to them. The women usually sang as they trekked back toward their homes. On that first outing, Mother taught them a song they had never heard before, and ever since, my Mother-Who-Chewed-on-Rope became known far and wide as the Poetess of the Mountain.

My uncle's scheme to see my parents married was a resounding success. Mother made a new man of Father, a man equal to any eventuality that might come his way. She came up with the idea that he should leave her in charge of things at home and try his luck as a merchant. Even the imam at the mosque had made a habit of saying that commerce was the key to the quasi totality of the world's riches. But commerce without money was an unthinkable proposition. Father had lived through the famine and dreaded living through that experience again. He knew of a man in a neighboring village, a usurer who kept his wife and child down to one meal a day. I can still see their ashen faces, the boy's dry lips, hard as wood. This usurer, everyone knew him as the Rock, agreed to lend Father the money he needed in exchange for a half share in the profits.

Father then embarked on a number of journeys into the mountains. The dangers he had to face were many and deadly; there were bandits and wild animals in those mountains, not to mention inclement weather. And sometimes we had to go for as long as two weeks without news of him. Every time he came home, he turned over half his profits to the Rock. His homecomings were always cause for celebration, but his days at home were fraught and much too few, and we never forgot that another trip was always looming around the corner.

Although these ventures meant that Father could finally have a little money for himself, for all of us, I remember him taking me aside one day to explain that the things he had learned and experienced on his travels were his most precious capital. Everywhere he went, he met people who became fast and true friends. Father liked to say he had built a castle on every mountain.

To Hizam's way of seeing things, illness was nothing but a lie and a way of shirking one's work, and work, as far as he was concerned, was the only surefire remedy against weakness and fatigue of any kind. Death was the only disease in his book. "If you feel ill, work, and God will heal you," he'd say to anyone who cared to listen. And in a way he was right: most illnesses do disappear by themselves. In our village, illness was the prerogative of those who could no longer move their limbs or had slipped into unconsciousness. Complaining or carrying on about one's aches and pains was not tolerated, period. Even in childbirth, women had to fend for themselves. Giving birth was just another twist in the daily round of farm and domestic chores. We faced illness much as animals did or trees or plants or insects, the only difference being that we liked to sing to speed the healing.

Then, to our great surprise, the government decided to open up a clinic in our village. We had to wait until the following year for the school. The Egyptian nurse who came to oversee the clinic was old, bearded, and pious, which is to say reliable. He began by offering his services to the imam and other village dignitaries. This proved to be an expedient way of winning the trust of everybody else, including the women. Everybody except for Hizam, who held the man personally responsible for bringing illness to the village.

One evening, Father invited the nurse over to our house. The minute he noticed the oozing sores all over Sister's feet, the nurse pushed his food away and immediately began rebuking Father. Father, it goes without saying, had already braved dangers of every kind to search for a remedy. He had traveled great distances, venturing high into the mountains and deep into the desert, even as far as far-off Yemen. The nurse, whom Father addressed as Doctor, explained that he was not a doctor and what Sister needed was help from the hospital in the city. Thanks to Father's new occupation, my parents now had the means to take Sister to the city for treatment. I was to stay behind in the care of my three sister-cousins. Because they knew Father and Mother didn't much trust the youngest one, who was amorous by nature, the two older ones left their husbands at home and came to take care of me.

During their stay, I was invited to a wedding along with every other man and boy in the village. Women were never asked to these things. The groom's family had slaughtered and boiled a bull for the event. The smell of meat seeped into houses up and down the street. Platters stacked high with meat were brought in, and specially "chosen" guests were entrusted with the delicate task of matching the right piece of meat to the right guest, according to the rules of rank and age.

Whatever was left over from this first go-around was handed out to the children.

On that day, I was given a large bone with a few shreds of meat still clinging to it and, happily, some marrow. It was the custom for guests to take some or all of the food offered at these festivities back home to their families. Chunks of meat were slipped into the folds of the *thob* and held in place against the belly by the belt, which doubled as a kind of pouch. I was determined to surprise my sister-cousins with my share of the takings. Aside from religious holidays, meat was a rare treat in the village. As soon as I stepped inside the house, I reached under my garment and pulled out the joint of meat and brandished it like a trophy. My sisters were so happy, so awed, so moved, so sure they couldn't have wished for a better brother, that they did not even dare reach for the meat, and one by one they came and kissed me. To them that bone became the most beautiful and unforgettable of gifts. And the gesture alone was enough to invest me with the necessary authority to become the man of the house.

A few days later, my parents and Sister came home. When Father heard all the stories about the bone, he decided to break with village custom and slaughter a sheep solely for his family's enjoyment, and for the first time ever, he asked me to assist him. Understand, that to me, this was a rebirth, a true birth. At long last, I was a man in Father's eyes—that's what his request meant.

From that moment on, tears, of course, were out of the question, and fear, too, come what may. Father waited until the next morning to give me the beautiful and brightly colored leather belt that held my first knife. Mother wept bittersweet tears and gazed at me with a longing that seemed to say I had left her arms forever. "Listen to me, son," she said. "You carry your maternal uncle within you. My family honor is now in your hands. And if the boy becomes a man, as the proverb says, it's because his maternal uncle became one before him." She asked me to always honor those words, and I felt such pride when I gave her my everlasting word that I would. In retrospect, I know I have not always been worthy, of either her family or mine.

The Other World

Every single norm we had ever lived by was turned on its head when they opened a school in our village. *They* prohibited us from carrying knives; *they* expected us to trim our nails and wear shoes and take up frequent bathing; *they* wanted us to mind the teachers recruited in Egypt, Jordan, and Syria. And whereas the village wanted to make me into the kind of man I could barely fathom, the ideas about life they were touting at the school seemed much better suited to my inner reality. I felt like a fish in water, and right from the start, I excelled. The school opened up ways of exploring the one thing the village and the tribe had tried to snuff out—my own subjective reality. There, language became a different thing; all the fields in the world could not have amounted to its vastness, its richness. There, I learned to touch words, all words, to read, write, and imagine them. There, we were simply children, no more, no less. There, courage was understood to mean something like authority and vulnerability and warmth and intelligence. There, it was absolutely forbidden to carry a knife. In short, it was a different world from Hizam's: a world where we could laugh and cry and speak and play, a world where we could be boys, not knives.

School gave me a soul and a language. I started compiling a dictionary of words I had never heard spoken in the village and of familiar words that until then had only had narrow meanings. Every word they taught us was a voyage in itself; the most beautiful words could be found in poems or in books of history and geography. *World* was one of those I liked best. Father didn't object when words became more important to me than the fields, but he drew the line when I took it into my head to teach everyone in the family how to read and write. "Ah, if only his sister had been the boy!" he lamented time and again.

Mother came upon me one day standing next to the watering hole, watching while the other boys swam. She wanted me to get in with the rest of them and learn, but I had a deadly fear of water, of the deep, deep hole, and wouldn't. Well, if I had no plans to join the others, she reasoned, then I should go home and help Sister with the housework. In the end, I learned how to swim—I had to if I was going to go on being a boy. Being a boy meant never failing. Even a dizzy spell rated as cowardice. Some of the fathers blamed the school for turning their sons into cowards and harbored suspicions of a government plot to drag the tribe down into everlasting depravation. A few even took their boys out of school, refusing to let them mix with anyone affiliated with the school. Hizam, on the other hand, surprised everybody by allowing his son to stay on, even though his virulent attacks on the institution didn't wane. I was the only one who gathered up the nerve to relay our general amazement. He explained that the only reason he had enrolled his son at the school was because of its connection to the founding monarch.

"But the founding monarch is long dead!" I said.

"Great men never die!" he countered.

Mercifully, our headmaster's people came from the village, and consequently, his authority was almost on a par with that of a village head, even though certain people viewed his family with undisguised contempt. His family had been among those that headed for the city during the famine. They held on to their lands and properties, however, and kept their ties to the village alive and never veered from a code of honor that considered all those who severed roots and sold off belongings as renegades. Everyone knew that in the cities they held jobs forbidden to tribesmen. We even heard about a man from a neighboring village who sold his house and his fields and then sent tradition to the winds by setting up as a butcher in the city. Trade in meat was for those who belonged to no tribe at all. In time, the man became so wealthy he could have bought himself a village if he wished, but he much preferred to gloat about how he had sold it all, every last thing he owned, even his share of wind.

Most of our fathers learned to read the Qur'an at Qur'-anic school. Once I asked Father to test me on a sura I was trying to learn by heart, but he hesitated when I handed him the book we used at school. When I saw him go in search of his old trusty copy, it suddenly dawned on me that he had memorized the verses and could only recognize them by the way they looked in his own Qur'an. After this incident, he took an even dimmer view of the school. Still, he couldn't hide his satisfaction that they had spared the traditional Qur'an, in other words his, out of respect for the true Qur'an, which could only be handled by those pure in body and soul.

Even in the days before the school opened its doors, the village had always had its own pedagogical system. For example, Mother taught me the three lessons of the cat that any man worth his salt should know: eat all your food, know your enemies, and hide your excrement. And the three lessons of the donkey: always drink your fill but never guzzle, carry your load, and know the way. Somehow, the headmaster managed to convince our fathers to place our welfare in the hands of the government; we were the sons of the state now and slated to rise as he had risen and become headmasters and officers and even ministers—who's to say? This last word was completely new to us. One day, our Arabic teacher asked us about our aspirations. I didn't hesitate to tell him I wished to be king. The boy sitting next to me, on the other hand, wished to live out his life and die surrounded by his flock of sheep.

Like all the other boys, I was expected to help in the fields before heading for school. Mother would have already fed the bull and brewed the coffee by the time Father came home from dawn prayers. I'd wake up, pray, and then Father, myself, and the bull would set off for the fields, all three of us barefoot. My school clothes and shoes were kept in a special bag, and the minute Mother came to take my place, I changed into them and went to school.

The school day began with all the boys lining up into rows. Every class was assigned its own teacher, whose duties included discipline and hygiene, the latter being particularly difficult as we always came straight from the fields. Every morning, as the school's top student, I had to present the flag—we now flew the country's flag instead of the tribal one. I pledged allegiance to the king, the crown prince, the minister of culture, and the members of the board of education, and all the other boys had to repeat after me. Our parents, in the meantime, were pledging allegiance to their fields.

The son of the village head turned up one day dressed in a pair of pants and a shirt that looked exactly like the ones worn by the teachers they had brought over from Egypt, Jordan, and Syria. His outfit took my breath away. I was filled with envy and begged Father to find me a similar suit of clothes. Father was ready to cater to my every whim—I was the school's top student, after all. He went to town and came back four days later with a shirt and a pair of pants he had bought off a soldier. I never managed to get the whole story out of him.

The next day, I arrived at the school before anyone else, all dressed up and looking like a foreigner. The entire family had pitched in to bring about my metamorphosis. When it was time to present the flag, I grabbed it and waved it with both hands, but with every shout of "Long live the King!" I could feel my pants slipping down another notch. The pants had a cloth belt, and we had tightened it as best we could and rolled up the legs many times over. By the time I got around to "Long live the Minister!" my pants were on the floor. And there I was, minus underwear, naturally. It was a good thing that the shirt, which was also several sizes too large, reached the middle of my thighs. The teacher quickly pulled up my pants and held them in place until I had finished the salutation. The next day, I went to school dressed in the usual way.

We all knew each other in the village. Everyone swam naked, the young and the old, and none of us had ever worn underwear. Hygienic facilities were nonexistent, and this posed a problem for the newcomers who wore pants. Even animals were afraid of these extraterrestrials. There were reports in the village that they had been seen peeing standing up, like devils. They slept late into the morning. Their food smelled strange. They bathed daily and blew their noses into hand-kerchiefs that they then stuck back into their pockets. Even their excrement was different because they ate eggs and vegetables and all kinds of things we had never heard of. They introduced us to the concept of garbage. We never used to throw away anything before they came along, except for ashes.

To the old-timers, the school might as well have been a war declared on them by the government. Our village was the only one that hadn't caved in to the Turks, and now look at it, this place of fierce resistance shamed into turning its children over to strangers! Other villages in the area referred to our village as *al watan*, the homeland; in fact, it was more like an em-pire. Almost all the villages in the area were under its protection. The welfare of entire villages, or at least of many families in those villages, was in the hands of cer-tain important families who lived in our village. The irony was that technically we didn't belong to the re-gion. Legend had it that our ancestor was from a dis-tant and mountainous land. He was one of seven war-mongering brothers. When news reached their father that his sons had slaughtered seven people in a single night, he resolved to punish them by sending them their separate ways and dispersing them forever. Our great ancestor settled in the area that later became known as our village and its outlying areas.

Now, this ancestor happened to have a very beautiful daughter who immediately caught the landowner's eye. The landowner tried to ply her father by offering every kind of dowry imaginable—money, livestock, even firearms—but the ancestor wanted land, and plenty of it, so that he could rid himself of the shame of being anyone's neighbor. Eventually, the two struck a deal. The groom-to-be and his bride would race one another. They would give the girl a bit of a head start, and the landowner would hand over any land she managed to cover before he caught up to her. The conditions were acceptable to the landowner, and the race took place with the ancestor as sole judge and arbiter. But the terrain was so vast, he soon lost sight of both his daughter and the landowner who was chasing after her. If it hadn't been for a thorn stopping her in her tracks, the girl would have covered the entire area and the groom demoted from owner to very distant neighbor!

They held the wedding, and now there is hardly a village in the region that can rival ours in terms of size. The ancient boundary lines have not changed to this day. Traces of enemy fire can still be seen on some walls. At home, we had documents attesting to a peace treaty my paternal grandfather, the village head in those days, had signed with the Turks. A time did come, however, when I stood by and watched Father burn all the papers because a friend had warned him about the dangers of having such documents under one's roof. The village imam did a similar thing with a manuscript of the Qur'an that had been kept in the mosque. He buried it in the ground when printed editions began arriving in great numbers. Assaults on village memory and history have not been few.

We had a daily date with the sun. Every morning, the whole village rose before sunrise. Really, we were the ones who roused the sun. Father used to say the sun was just another one of our work tools. Even clouds never managed to completely obscure it; even when rain fell, the sun shone bright. The sun cleansed us and gave us renewed strength every day.

We had our own notions about hygiene in the village. But when the school decided to institute a day of cleanliness, every family went into a frenzy of activity. The headmaster designated Saturdays as the day when we would be put to the test. The new measures had been implemented with the utmost seriousness, and the school promised a prize to the family with the cleanest boy.

My parents decided to entrust me to Sister. On the appointed Friday morning, we scaled a mountain in search of water. It was freezing that morning. Sister undressed me and started to scrub me with a fairly large stone she kept dipping into the ice-cold water. In the name of glory and for the sake of the school, I withstood the numbing cold and the stone scraping away at my flesh. Come Saturday morning, there were only three boys who even qualified for the contest. But I saw the prize go to one of my cousins, no doubt because his sister was more beautiful than mine and because he had been bathed with soap. Well, that was a village first! Later, the teacher was made to pay dearly for his choice. There were rumors about him favoring the boy, and his every move was subjected to round-the-clock vigilance. In the end, he had to leave the village, which also meant the school, and, as a result, the school's first hygiene prize was also the last!

The men usually washed up at the mosque, where there was a contraption that worked as a kind of shower. They filled the tank with water and tilted it so it would flow out in a slow stream. Anyone who bathed before morning prayers was implicitly admitting to a night of lovemaking. And even if they had made love with most of their clothes on, they had to wash themselves from head to toe in order to be fit for prayer.

Mother had already instructed me on the dangers of naked lovemaking and warned me about the earth-scorching heat that emanated from a woman's breasts. She swore up and down that a man from her village had put this phenomenon to the test, and here was proof if I wanted it. First, he slaughtered a sheep, and, moving quickly, he stripped it of its hide, which he then placed over his naked wife. After the two made love, he observed that the pelt was scorched from top to bottom! This irrefutable evidence of female heat was displayed in the marketplace, where it remained for many months.

Every time I came home with good grades, Father would gleefully rub his hands and say, "It's happening. It's happening. It's getting closer by the day!" Then, he would kiss my mother. Around the time of my birth, he had a dream about a very tiny light that kept growing and growing until it filled the entire earth. The village imam had interpreted this to mean that he would give birth to a son whose light would radiate throughout the world.

Although Father may have seen me as a dream on the verge of coming true, Mother, the more realistic of the two, often saw me as a nightmare! The one time I hit Sister, she swore I wouldn't escape punishment. I knew it was useless to appeal to Father, so I ran straight to the woman whose wish was to kiss me for all the days of her life and told her I had been sent by Mother to invite her and her five children over for dinner. She had already cooked her evening meal and didn't really take my invitation seriously. But I wouldn't budge from her door and told her Mother was sure to beat me if I went home without her. I finally convinced her Mother was expecting us, and she agreed to come, all the time telling me how she felt so blessed to have such good neighbors. Mother opened the door and let out a small cry of surprise, which the neighbor immediately mistook for pleasure. Father rushed off to slaughter our one and only rooster, whose song at daybreak had been as reliable as a call to prayer.

Never in my life had I seen Mother behave the way she did that evening. Whenever I had been upset in the past, I would shun my food and fake sleepiness, but Mother always persuaded me to stay and eat my meal. But on this night she spent all her time asking me if I wasn't sleepy, and I spent all mine pretending I hadn't heard her.

All four of us slept in the same room then. Father slept off to one side with his knife by his head, and Mother, Sister, and I shared the other bed. When our neighbor left, Father wished me a good night as he always did. But I found it hard to sleep without Mother's smell in the room. Finally, I got up and went out to join her on the roof terrace, up high near the stars and sky. She was singing. I have always thought stars were really words that Mother could pluck out of the sky to fashion into songs. It didn't take me long to understand that this night they were going to be my punishment. Mother knew how susceptible I was to songs. I started crying and promised never to hit Sister again. "Sister is a song. How can anyone have ill will toward a song?" said Father, who was also having trouble sleeping and had come out to join us on the roof, high up near the stars and sky.

In the village, every activity had its special song. No one ever did anything without singing. We sang for everything—as if nothing could live or grow or be completed without poetry. We sang so that life would dance, and often it did.

Mother once told me that in the beginning, our village was a song, unique as the sun, unique as the moon. And there are certain words, with a special poetic power, that can take wing like butterflies, and the most beautiful and colorful ones are the lightest of all. What better place than our village, therefore, perched so near the sky, as everyone knows, for the words to show themselves and illuminate the earth with their light? "Everything is a poem," Mother used to say, "the trees, the plants, the flowers, the rocks, water . . . If you listen closely to things, you can hear them singing."

This is how things have been since our ancestors tilled their first field. Their voices were mingled with the earth like fertilizer, and I have no doubt that all the natural riches people talk about were born of that union. Children are bathed in song from birth; they are steeped in songs that settle deep within them. The dead we bury are turned into songs. Even Hizam agrees with my mother on this last point.

"I know our ancestors sang even while they slept," Hizam used to say, "but they only sang about the virtues of work. The *Tarafs* were the ones who brought poetry to the fields. *Tarafs* have no ties to the land and no one knows where they came from. They're free to sing about anything and everything—rain, journeys, slavery, love, sadness, hospitality, or anything they please. Unfortunately, some of them have gone so far as to use song as a kind of blackmail. They stand in the doorways of those who refuse them entry and insult them in front of the whole tribe. They're the reason poetry has lost its nobility. I've witnessed it firsthand and that's why I don't sing anymore. Then there are those like your mother who will stand up for the *Tarafs* and say that now people work the land better than ever before, with greater joy, with a pleasure they never knew before. There's some truth in it, but what I really hold against the *Tarafs* is that they brought us dancing and colorful clothing and henna and coffee and sugar and work tools and carpets and, worst of all, keys and locked doors. Who bothered with locked doors before they came? Also, men and women are the same to them. They're not at all like us, made from entirely different stuff. Remember that man, the one they said nursed his own daughter. They are a group unto themselves, and there isn't one tribe that doesn't acknowledge their singularity, their ability to roam free, in peace and without fear. All they need is a black flag surmounted by a rooster's head and they're off; whereas the rest of us have to remain cloistered in our homes or risk our lives every time we cut across an enemy's fields. Every time I hear your father say that our tribe wouldn't amount to a thing without them, it sends a chill down my spine. Even though I know he spent all his time as a young man singing and dancing with the *Tarafs,* moving with them from village to village, going from one wedding feast to the next."

"Well, at school they taught us all Muslims are equal."

"Go tell that to your father, he'll be overjoyed."

"But the *Tarafs* are handsome, their daughters beautiful, and they eat and dress better than us, and there are generous people among them, much more generous than many in our tribe."

Even though there were love stories between their world and ours, these never ended in marriage. "We are married to our fields," Hizam used to say. "Our roots are in the earth, but they're made of wind. How can you expect to marry the wind?"

While Hizam and I sat chatting one day, the village shopkeeper's wife came by to sell him some henna for his daughter. The smell emanating from her hair and body and clothing was exquisite.

"I don't understand how beauty can be fashioned," Hizam protested. "One is either beautiful or not, and nothing is as beautiful as nature's handiwork." For Hizam, words only meant what he wanted them to.

When I realized this, I vowed always to wipe words clean before uttering them. Mother used to say human beings should have necks as long as camels so that they can clean their words, which sometimes can be just as dangerous as bullets.

There was a legend in our village that said that the true poet is the one who is awakened by djinns in the middle of the night and offered a bowl of milk filled with hairs. Anyone who drinks this offering becomes a poet. I tended to believe another legend, one I heard from Father. There was a bounty of snakes in the village, he said: angel snakes, racing snakes, and black snakes. Angels raised their heads very high whenever they crossed paths with human beings, and one had to take great care not to kill them as this was their way of signaling they were at peace with humankind. If a black snake, on the other hand, fails to kill a human being, it kills itself on the spot. So, snakes are the ones who taught us how to tell war from peace. When a man passes another man without raising his head or greeting him, his behavior is seen as an affront.

Some nights, Father would call me and show me the light that shone from the ruins of a village that had long since disappeared. The light, he said, came from inside the mouth of a snake that was standing guard over lost and ancient treasures. There were rumors in the village about men who woke up in the dead of night, not to drink milk and become poets, but to hunt for buried treasure. Only those who went in search of it without feeling any fear and brought it back without casting a single backward glance would be allowed to keep the treasure.

The legend also said that God only laughs when a woman and a snake cross paths, because each one is afraid of the other.

My Sisters My Memory

I had six sisters then, my real sister, the one I call My-Sister-My-Memory, two half sisters on my mother's side, My-Sister-Who-Loves-Me and My-Sister-Whom-I Love, and three sister-cousins: My-Sister-Father, My-Sister-Mother, and My-Sister-I. Only my mother knew that I called them by these names. Later, there would be two more, my father's daughters from his second marriage, and they were my Sister-Daughters. Today, as I write, I am eight sisters rich.

I was also a *samyy*, a godfather to eight boys who had been named after me. It was customary in our village for children to bear the names of individuals who had been entrusted with their welfare. One of the eight was Hizam's own son. These days, Hizam's date and raisin munching is worse than ever; even during prayers, even at the mosque, he munches. Hizam is having a hard time dying. He can't let go of the past, and he's never really adapted to all the changes. He is the only survivor of a generation that is long gone, and when he was told I now live in Paris, he cursed the day the school came to disrupt our village ways. One of his reasons for not liking the school, he once told me, was that the teachers were always impeccably shaved. In Hizam's eyes, a man without a beard was by definition a liar. All tribesmen saw beards as tokens of honesty and sincerity. So, as far as Hizam was concerned, beardless men were no better than mannish women!

Hizam's intransigence was hardly news to me. Recriminations were always in order whenever he came across a boy who had neglected to wear his knife and belt. A man's belly, he thought, should be as flat as a wolf's. His own feet had never known shoes, and he refused to be separated by even so much as a sliver of leather from the earth on which he trod. Nothing irked him more than lovesickness or people going on about their aches and pains. He couldn't stand the sight of us lazing about in the shade of a tree or eating more than our fill or sleeping late into the morning or laughing too loud. Even something as harmless as a stroll was anathema to him. But nothing pained him more than seeing a young man seated at the wheel of a car. We always took great pains so he wouldn't find out that we had taken an airplane or slept in a hotel or eaten in a restaurant. He mocked anyone who tried to speak of the world, especially Egypt and Egyptians, whom he held directly responsible for the school and all the catastrophes that came with it. The first time Father bought us rice and onions, Hizam rushed to criticize him and accuse him of undermining tradition.

And when it came to women, Hizam felt nothing but disdain. He never missed a chance to make a case for the superiority of the triumphant male. He knew every boy in the village but not a single girl. We were all terrified of him, especially the women. How could we live in peace with him around? Even at the mosque, where he was always the first to arrive, not so much to pray as to keep an eye on us, we couldn't breathe freely. The mosque, he insisted, would always remain the last line of defense.

Although Hizam rarely spoke, the faces and gestures he made spoke louder than words. Only rain and nature were to his taste. The very idea of rest was alien to him. Even in the dead of night, one could hear noises coming from the ground floor of his house. There was a rumor circulating about the great treasure he had amassed and the long nights he spent counting his fantastic riches over and over again. Some even claimed to have heard the sound of nighttime digging coming from deep within the house. Or at least that's what we were told by the young men who amused themselves on their late walks home after a night of dancing by listening under the windows of married folk, especially newlyweds. This was an old, old custom in the village, and young men routinely scaled the walls of a bridegroom's

house to eavesdrop on the bride's virginal cries and
her young husband's valiant response. The whole village would turn up early the next morning to study the
bridegroom's face for traces of the battle he had waged
during the night and to see if the young bride held her
legs far apart when she walked and if her nightdress,
hastily washed of telltale blood, had been hung out
on the roof to dry. Family and friends basked in a self-
congratulatory haze, especially the bride's mother, who
could now brag that her daughter had been raised in the
purest tradition. To express his approval of women who
were virgins on their wedding night, Hizam wished
the new brides a good morning, after which they could
rest assured he would never again address them in his
lifetime.

Every single one of my sisters did the family proud,
and Mother had nothing to be ashamed of, not even
with the eldest, whose marriage was an arranged one.
Her father, the stingy rich man, had insisted she marry
against her will a certain boy from a well-to-do family.
From the start, her heart was set against this man, and
on the first night of the festivities, she waited until all
the men had gathered at the dinner table to escape from
her husband's house. The darkness and the mountains
did not deter her as she bravely made her way to the
house of my maternal uncle, who took her in until such
time as she could divorce. Later, she married another
man who was very much like my father, and she has

been as lucky in love as Mother. Her new husband had little in the way of possessions, a few uncultivated fields at best, but she rose to the challenge. In time their luck changed, and they now have two daughters and four sons, the same number of children as Mother, but not as many as my other sisters.

In the clinic where he worked, her husband met a woman with whom he fell in love. My sister soon noticed that something was up. He was coming home later than usual, and in the mornings he dressed with greater care and used perfume and sang. Before long, the rumors began. He came home one night just as the sun was setting to find the front door bolted. He called out to his wife and received no answer. When his calling turned to shouting, every ear and window in the village opened wide.

"Go, go home to her, now. Everybody knows you love her and she loves you. This is my house now, and you don't stand much of a chance of ever setting foot in it again."

He warned that he would go to her father, the man who had fathered seven sons and had, at one time, been married to my mother. My sister, who did not scare easily, told him to make sure he didn't forget to omit the part about being in love. My brother-in-law got into his car and drove straight to his father-in-law's house. Sadly, Mother was already dead or she would have been proud, even more so than I was of my sister that day.

Her father gave orders for a sheep to be slaughtered and sent two of his sons to bring his daughter to him. She didn't even bother to speak to them, and they returned home empty-handed. When the gravity of the situation dawned on him, her father took his son-in-law and when they reached his daughter's house, he said, "Daughter, I bring you your wife."

My brother-in-law stood on the threshold and gave her his word he would never cheat again. She opened the door, and the village closed its ears and windows once more.

A Week in the City

At school we learned that the Prophet had urged all Muslims to go in search of knowledge, to pursue it from the cradle to the grave. Even if it meant going as far away as far-off China. This school that was cutting us off from our village was now prompting us to journey, we who had never so much as met the people in the next village. But even those strangers were not quite so foreign as the words they were teaching us at school. We were learning classical Arabic, a strange language full of words no villager had ever heard. As a result, I acquired a vast vocabulary I didn't entirely understand and that was hardly of any use as far as village life was concerned. Still, my composition teacher, impressed by my abilities, advised my father to buy me newspapers so that I could hone what he called my leisure reading.

Friday is a sacred day to Muslims everywhere, a holy day that also happened to be market day in our village. On Fridays, Father bought us meat and honey. He fed my sister and me slivers of raw liver, kidneys, and a little honey, a delicacy usually served only to guests. Most families ate meat at their Friday dinner, but a few were too poor even for that. Mother always held a few pieces of meat in reserve for people in the neighborhood who had to do without, and Father always turned a blind eye. By the time we were in our sixth year of schooling, our headmaster resolved that it was high time for us to obtain valid birth certificates and identity cards, documents that could only be had in the city. By virtue of having read two issues of a magazine published by the largest petrochemical company in the country (Father had bought them off a former employee of the company on one of his market-day forays), I came to be seen as the most worldly member in our little group. We all piled into the car that made the weekly Saturday run to the city and embarked on our journey. I had forewarned my fellow travelers that we would see people—even women—in trousers. I had this valuable information from my godfather, who worked as a driver for the Pakistani doctor who was going to help us establish our real birth dates. Our fathers found the car ride excruciating; they were, without exception, sick to their stomachs and none so sick as Hizam, who spent the entire journey cursing the school with renewed zeal.

Those without friends or relatives in the city lodged in boarding houses run by widows. Father and I stayed with our cousin, the former headmaster of the village school. It had not been for lack of trying, but during his tenure as headmaster, this good man only managed to convince the village to open up a school for boys. And as he did not want to deprive his daughters of the benefits of an education, he had found no other recourse than to send them to study alongside the boys. He tried to rally other fathers to follow suit, but to no avail. In the end, he had to resign himself to the fact that his daughters did not belong in that school and that his love for the village did not entitle him to sacrifice their future welfare. Hizam, who already took a dim view of this man for belonging to a family that talked too much without saying anything, never forgave him for sending his girls to school with boys, or for introducing the rest of us to a world we never knew existed and thereby changing our lives forever.

We were hosted by our cousin for a week. If it hadn't been for Hizam, who was still waiting for his ID, we could have left as early as Tuesday when the car that had delivered us made its return trip. Furthermore, how was Hizam's son to obtain his documents if his father didn't have any? Our cousin, who felt somewhat responsible for all these new upheavals in our lives, took it upon himself to help Hizam get the necessary papers.

The minute we stepped into the hospital we saw women wearing trousers and a doctor who barely spoke Arabic . . . in other words, extraterrestrials as far as Hizam was concerned. And even though prayers were still hours away, he dashed off to the mosque by himself and then spent the rest of the day talking about the end of the world and the fall of the government. Every time a female nurse came anywhere in his vicinity, he spat on the floor. One of the nurses, resolving to put an end to this unacceptable behavior, came and took him by the arm and showed him the door. He allowed himself to be led like a child, this man whom no woman had ever touched.

"Was her hand hot?" I wanted to know. "You know they're going to have to undress us and even touch our peckers to figure out how old we are."

"Rape us, you mean!" He shooed me away as he spoke. "You can tell my son that if he lets them have their way with him, he can forget he ever had a father, and you may as well know, I sorely regret the day I decided to name him after you."

When his son finally emerged from the examination room looking a bit peaked, Hizam undressed him then and there in front of everyone, and when he was reassured all was as it should be, he burst into tears and held his son to him for a long while. Father walked out of his own checkup and came over in a state of semi-undress to console his friend:

"Did you know that nurse fell in love with you? She says you remind her of her father, especially the beard. And she asked me to ask you to remove your belt and knife and come into the room with me so she can examine you."

Hizam immediately placed his hand on his knife, ready to defend himself at any cost.

"Go tell her I am not a schoolboy. I am a married man, and I have no intention of taking a second wife, least of all a Christian one."

"But she's not Christian at all, she's Muslim. A Muslim woman from Pakistan. They're all Muslims over there in Pakistan, and the men have beards that are even longer and bushier than yours."

"What? You think she'd want to come live with me in the village? Do you think my wife would agree to take her in?"

"Actually, she thought it would be much better if you came to live with her in the city, and then later she could take you back with her to Pakistan."

"Oh, brother, my brother, please take me back to my village. This place is going to be the death of me, I can tell."

But my father wouldn't let up and kept on teasing him.

"She says you're gentle and as well behaved as a child. Even women, she says, are not as well behaved. She says you're the perfect man, the ideal man. But if you don't want to have anything to do with her, be very careful, because they have ways of keeping us here, even against our will."

And just then, the nurse appeared. She had come to

apologize to Hizam and brought a policeman along to interpret. The sight of them struck panic in the old man's heart. Calling up all his strength, he hurtled out of there, vaulted over the wall, and landed in the graveyard that bordered the hospital. Much later, we came upon him at the mosque, and he beseeched us not to breathe a word about his mishaps in the city to anyone in the village, especially not a word to the women.

Our week in the city was a terrible one for Hizam. For one thing, he hated bathrooms and wanted nothing more than to go home to his immaculate house and to his village without toilets. But more than anything, he fretted about his fields, his bull, his livestock. He was worried his wife would oversleep and leave his land unguarded for others to take advantage of.

At our cousin's house, they served us rice at every meal. We all ate it, except for his mother, who was as old as Hizam and who would only eat bread baked the village way. The two of them sat off to one side, dipping their bread into melted butter and honey and chattering away. Hizam, who couldn't stand rice, would periodically break away from their heart-to-heart to inform us that "rice swells the belly and bloats the thighs, and when there's tomato sauce in the picture, then you're really pushing your luck . . ."

The old woman was the first person in the village to wear reading glasses. Hizam wanted to know if she had purchased them in Mecca.

"No, I went to a local doctor."

"I mean for the glasses."

"For the glasses, yes."

"To what tribe does this doctor belong?"

Our cousin tried to explain. "Doctors are people like us," he said. "They learn about medicine in schools, big schools we call universities. Who knows? Maybe some-day one of these boys you see eating here will become a doctor and help take care of us."

"God willing! God willing! Only God can cure all ills!" Hizam concluded.

His trip ended in a searing failure. His son, like me, wasn't old enough to qualify for an identity card, and the doctor who was in charge was not about to bend the rules and even refused to listen to his own driver. These cards, we found out, were only issued to eighteen-year-olds. I could hardly believe my ears at the many lies my father told that day in order to convince the doctor I was much older than my years. When we presented ourselves at the branch where the cards were dispensed, the policeman who was studying our files addressed himself directly to Father:

"You're no better than an ox. All you need is a tail and a pair of horns!"

"Listen, we've left no stone unturned. Even our cousin, who's the doctor's personal driver, in case you don't know, tried to put in a good word for us. He's not a nobody, after all; that's an important post. Well, nothing. I'm telling you this doctor has no respect for our tribe."

"Calm down," the policeman urged. "All of you calm down. Can't you see the doctor is already breaking the law?"

"You see! I told you he has no respect for the tribe."

"And why should he?"

At which point every man present went for his knife.

"But I am one of you, I come from the same tribe," the policeman assuaged us. "But things have changed. Life is not what it used to be. And it's better if our children are younger. The younger the better. So they can accrue many years of work before they have to retire."

Hizam took his son by the hand, stepped up to the policeman, and planted a kiss on the man's beard.

"You are my son," he said, "and I am your father. And you see this boy here, he's your little brother, as are all these other boys. For a week now, we've been lost in this city without food or shelter, and all this time, I have been without news of the village."

In the end, Hizam managed to win the policeman over, and there were those in our group who came away from the city with their IDs in hand. The younger boys, myself included, were given birth certificates that made no mention of their true date of birth.

A week after our return to the village, a pious man informed us that in one of his pronouncements, the

Prophet had urged the separation of males and females after the age of ten. At home, Mother, My-Sister-My-Memory, and I always slept side by side, with Father sleeping nearby. How else were we to get through the icy nights up there, three thousand meters above the plain? Father listened carefully to the man and then said something to the effect that I was getting too old.

"But she's my mother!"

"You can sleep with me."

"Does this mean Hizam can't sleep with his wife anymore?"

"You haven't understood a thing. They're married."

Mother wasn't too strict about implementing this new rule. She still kept me warm and waited for me to doze off before going to lie down next to my sister. She tried to keep both God and her son happy. My sister was allowed to stay put, alongside the one who was our Mother both by day and by night, but a new sadness crept over her. God, she said, was keeping us apart. I did what I could to cheer myself up by claiming I was a man now.

Most of all, I missed my mother's warmth, her poetic presence. This was not lost on her, and bedtime was pushed off to a later and later hour. We spent a great part of the night singing by the fire, telling stories about love, and reciting all the poems I ended up learning by heart. My mother filled all of me with poetry and fire.

The Rainbow

A day came when I had to confess my love for another woman to my mother.

"You know how I love poetry, Mother, and how I love you even more than I love poetry ... but this girl has something more than you and poetry put together. I am certain she's the one, the Rainbow."

Hizam had entrusted me with one of the village's deep-down secrets. The first poem that ever was, he said, came into being in our village. In the beginning it came as a plant, a plant awash in a thousand shades of color, each color fragrant with a thousand scents and each scent enclosing a thousand souls. Our forebears were a primeval, fruitful soil, and the words they spoke came forth in the form of souls. They would stand naked as trees under the falling rain. Then, for many months on end, the waters began to rise, and everywhere one turned, the women were pregnant. Never had anyone seen such a thing. United by this strange predicament, the women later dallied and refused to return to the fields so soon after giving birth. Their refusal whetted the anger of their men, but the women were adamant. "You have your plants," they said, "and we have ours!" The men took this mass desertion as a sure sign of female weakness and agreed to carry water back to the new mothers, but never without a hint of disdain and a show of superiority.

In all likelihood, the women would have overlooked the petty ways of their men were it not for the events that were to follow. "There's no water in the water!" The terrible cry went up one day as if announcing the end of the world. The water the men brought back was unequal to nourishing or slaking the thirst of the poetic plants. The plants fled the village and made for the sky, where they were transformed into clouds and lightning bolts and storms . . . Never had anyone seen such clashing. Rains such as those, deadly rains, downpours of rocks and pebbles, had never fallen on human beings before. Our ancestors mustered what little strength they could and began to sing. And when the sun beheld their terrible struggle, it intervened. Extending its left hand over the village for protection, it gathered up all the plants with its right hand and set them down in the form of a beautiful woman, the most beautiful woman in the village, the one who to this day is known as the Rainbow.

And it was then that water lost its single most important trait. It no longer gave things their true color;

instead, it wore the color things gave it and was not the color of water at all. If water were ever to regain its original powers, the women reasoned, then they had better be the ones in charge of drawing and fetching it. To meet this enormous challenge, they divided into two groups—while some of them went in search of water, others stayed behind to nurse the children. Even though they went to the greatest lengths, they were, in the end, unable to save the water; instead, they created the milk bond that would turn all children into brethren. The village was once again one enormous family. The first water of the ancients became the light of day, because it retained its essential ability to endow things with color. To this day, in the village, one can still see water running down the throat of a rainbow.

Hizam also told me another version of the story in which our village was the first place on earth to witness love between a man and a woman. But things got so out of hand that countless couples who could no longer withstand the intensity of the love they felt killed themselves or died from having loved too much. Love itself was on the brink of death, because only those who had not loved survived. And again, the sun stepped in and saved both love and human life by turning love into a rainbow.

"Now you understand why I am still alive, child," Hizam concluded. "But in the end, it's all a lot of claptrap. I'll tell you what I really think. There's only one

thing that gives men and women their form and color
and things their beauty, and that's tilling the soil."

"What about water?"

"There's plenty of water. You just have to dig a little
and you'll find it. Drought is a scourge only in countries
where people sleep too much."

For Mother, poetry took over where water left off;
only poetry could bring color to things and beings. It
took a true poet to recognize the energies and powers
water had never lost. Especially water that collects in
the eye, there where our real truth appears in a shim-
mer of colors.

My Rainbow once told me about the time she saw
my reflection in a well and how she drank and drank of
that water until she was certain she had drunk me all
up. I was crazy with love for her after that. This was the
first time in her life she was declaring her love for anyone. I confided in an old woman from the village. She
counseled me to steal seven hairs from my Rainbow
love and to gather seven pebbles that had touched her
feet and to place these together with a sura from the
Qur'an somewhere in the vicinity of the door to her
house. But Mother caught me with pebbles in hand.

"Who told you to do this? That old woman who
never loved or married even though she tried every
trick in the book? I know you are terribly in love, but
you've just tossed the last of your milk teeth to the sun

and if it's suffering you're after, you have all of your life ahead of you."

It was a village tradition for children to hurl their milk teeth at the sun. Technically, one was supposed to aim for the eye of the sun and accompany the offering with a request for adult teeth as everlasting as sunlight.

Father, too, had gotten wind of my condition. His solution was to teach me how to swim. He stopped going to the neighborhood mosque and went instead to a mosque in my Rainbow's neighborhood. The idea that one could switch mosques had never even occurred to me before. I followed in Father's footsteps and was soon praying at the new mosque with a humility that even my elders could not match. They took me in as one of their own, until I overdid it as usual. Alarmed by my zeal, my Rainbow's father called on my parents to alert them to my strange behavior and suggest they keep an eye on me. Overhearing what he had to say about me was enough to bring my praying days at his mosque to an end.

For two whole weeks I avoided her. I had to come up with some new way of being exceptional before I could even contemplate showing myself to her. My family owned a beautiful she-donkey, more or less on a par with what a Ferrari or powerful racing motorcycle would be today. And I knew the secret that could make her fly like

the wind. At that hour of the day when the sun is about
to set, the sun of the dead we called it, and plummet into
the sea to guzzle it down, I rode my donkey past my
Rainbow's house. She was there on the terrace with her
mother. A light touch of the switch to the rump, and
my mount would take off like the wind. I so wanted my
Rainbow to be awed by my hidden talents, but my ef-
forts were brought to a crashing halt when a pit viper
reared up out of nowhere, catching me off guard. I
tumbled to the ground and came very close to being
trampled by my donkey as she trotted off homeward.
Humiliated yet again, I now had no doubt that I had
lost all credibility in my beloved's eyes. I hid for a few
days. Mother, who was keeping a close eye on my jabs
at freedom, advised me to sing. As far as she was concerned, this was the one thing at which I excelled.
Hizam, who loved me as he would his own son and
knew how utterly I trusted him, was also full of ideas on
how I should proceed. He also advised singing, but only
on one condition. First, I would have to see the sun
shine bright in the dead of night.

"The first lovers on earth were Sun and Moon.
That's what they say, anyway. Sun was the woman and
Moon her husband. They loved one another to distrac-
tion. Love was the only light on earth and between the
pair of them, they had used it all up. A dark night fell
over the earth, but this did not affect them as they could
still make one another out and see other things in their

immediate vicinity. They had many children in every color known to man and all born with their eyes shut. In order to save their children, to say nothing of the rest of the world, they had to give some light back. And that's what they decided to do. Father Moon rushed to offer himself up, but Mother Sun pointed out that she had more light to spare, and together they came up with the idea of sharing the task. And that, my boy, is how we came to have night and day. Mother Sun was nursing her newest born just then. She held him to her breast while she turned herself into the Sun, and that's how our village ended up perched so high, near the sky. And that's still true to this day. Every now and then, we think she is hiding from us and we feel consumed by the fear of an impending disaster. But, like any mother, she too likes to come down and be among her children. She will stop somewhere to nurse a child, usually a boy, occasionally a girl, and later, these children will become singers of the light."

I asked Hizam about those who say it is the Moon who is the woman.

"That's your mother speaking!" he said. "Get out of my sight, you mollycoddled mama's boy. Every woman I know has sun in her, I'm sure of it. Can't you see how luminous they all are? And that's why I steer clear of them—you can get burned by the sun!"

"But how can I be expected to see the sun at night when it spends its nights guzzling down the ocean?"

"The sun burns all day, and at night it disappears behind that mountain and drinks up the ocean, but then it turns into a woman in the shape of a star. All those who've seen her say she is the most beautiful by far. She journeys across the sky, moving from east to west. If you're lucky enough to see her, then the Rainbow will be yours. There's no other way."

I knew I was much too old to be nursed as a sun-child, and my chances of becoming a real poet were quite slim. My only chance was to somehow see the sun in the dead of night, and I was going to take it. Our neighbor was an old woman who never slept and spent all her time talking to herself. She knew every profanity in the village backwards and forwards. In fact, she knew them so well that My-Sister-My-Memory and I believed she was the wellspring of every foul curse that had ever been uttered. Whenever she went to stand up, she farted and the two of us would be overcome by end-less fits of giggling. Overhearing us, she would shout, "Stop that or I'll come after you, you worthless shit-eating flies!" I sat up with this old woman for several nights running. We were no longer on the lookout for the sun. Instead, she taught me every curse in the book and told me about the exploits of this one and the mishaps of that one, making me privy to every true and false secret in the village and showing me all of its seamy underside. No one was spared, except for Mother. I suppose this was because Mother went behind Father's back to give the old woman milk and butter every night and never had anything bad to say about anyone.

In the end, I completely forgot about the sun. I learned the hidden history of the village instead and began to see all the people around me in a very different light. Whenever I came upon this one or that one, I couldn't help but laugh. Of course, I couldn't confront anyone with the truth because their truth was also mine. We were all one in the village, and whatever may have touched any one of us applied to the rest as well. Even the houses were joined like cousins, each with its two doors—one opening onto the ground floor and a second one onto the roof. Anyone could walk the entire length of the village simply by moving from one roof to the next.

When the villagers added it all up—my zeal at prayers, my debacle with the she-donkey, and, most recently, my uncontrollable fits of laughter—they concluded I was mad like my cousin before me. Everyone in the village remembered the Saturday afternoon when all the men were off at market in a neighboring village and my cousin jumped stark naked from a fifth-floor window. And how he shot across the fields as though he had wings even though the fields were under water. Mother saved the family honor that day, the honor of the entire village, in fact, by having the wherewithal to catch up to him. With the help of an extraordinarily pretty girl, she lured him back to the house, and later, when the men returned from market, they raised a white flag in honor of the two women.

Even the old woman turned on me, denying she had ever told me any of the things she had. People in the village went out of their way to avoid me, except for my Rainbow.

"If only you could stay small forever so that I could spend the rest of my life looking into your eyes."

"That won't happen. We Rainbows are only allowed one mistake. What if I loved you and you didn't turn out to be a true poet? I would be condemned to die."

Few are the times I've looked into a woman's eyes. Even though Father always told me it is far more important to see a woman than to look at her. I've never been that brave. As always, I ran to Hizam. As always, he blamed my mother, poetry, and the school, and the two of us wept together.

"I've never seen you smile, Father Hizam."

"Well, my mouth is busy most of the time. And really, it's not up to me at all. If I took up smiling, I'd probably never do another honest day's work in my life. And I do smile, at least twice a year I smile, when we bring in the harvest. Anyway, I'm running out of smiles and can't go around wasting them right and left."

"Why? Is there a predetermined number you can't go beyond?"

"Oh, it's much worse than that. I've been allotted a

lifetime supply of smiles, and it is our sacred tradition in this village never to overshoot that number."

"What sacred tradition?"

"Ever since Yalaa was killed."

"Yalaa our ancestor?"

"No, not that Yalaa, another Yalaa. An infant who bore the same name as our ancestor and was killed on account of a smile. A very long time ago, there was a slaughter, a feud between two families. That very same night, the killers went calling on the grieving relatives of those they had killed. They came to gloat over the sadness they had inflicted, but instead, they found smiling faces and people behaving as if the killing had never taken place. They went back to their homes and sought out an old witch, as mean as that neighbor of yours. Smiles, she told them, would always reign in a house where there was a baby. And then those evil men returned and killed that family's smile forever. Ever since that time, the village has rationed out a set number of smiles for each of us, and only I know how many, and I'm the only one who follows the rule."

Mother's version had a few additional twists. To her knowledge, we each had a specific number of smiles set aside for us, but no one could say for sure how many were allotted to each person. In the old days, when people still knew their allotted number, they discovered that if they saved their last smile for a tree, say, it would instantly become a fruit-bearing tree—naturally, this was long before there were any fruit-bearing trees. A woman's last smile gave sweet fruit, and a man's slightly sour ones. The last smiles of children yielded countless kinds of vegetables and spices and flowers! As for Hizam, I'm sure he doesn't have the faintest idea how many smiles each one is allotted, and his must have run out a very long time ago.

It began to rain on us. Hizam was working butter into my hair. I had fallen asleep. My head rested on his thigh while he sat listening to the song of the fields in the rain, the only song that met with his approval. When I woke up, the Rainbow appeared to me in all her beauty. I was saved, not mad at all, and if I stopped singing, I would become a man. Like birds descending on a field after rainfall, I too wanted to protect the one dearest to my heart. I went to my special rock, smooth and wide as a warm and humid bed. I soon went back to sleep and for the first time saw the sun set in the east. It must have been the middle of the night, when I woke up to find myself astride my mother's back. She had gone looking for me and found me. Apparently, in the village they were already saying the mad boy had disappeared. I told Mother I had seen the sun setting in the east.

"And the Rainbow, I saw the Rainbow!"

"The real one?"

"Yes, the real one."

"No, I mean *your* Rainbow?"

"No, Mother, no."

"Why didn't you sing as I told you to?"

"I won't be singing anymore, Mother. I want to become a man."

"But how can you be you if you don't sing?"

"And what about madness?"

"If you think it's singing that drives people mad, then you must make sure never to stop singing. Look at me. Is your mother mad?"

"No."

"And I'm always singing."

There was feasting at our house that night. My homecoming was celebrated by all. I was heartened to see they weren't flying the white flag this time. There was some wagging of tongues, of course, and whispering about Mother's special gift for luring the mad back to their homes. My-Sister-My-Memory was the only one who spoke to me as she always had before. To show her how thankful I felt, I told her she was my real rainbow.

I decided to play along, to beat them at their own game. If they wanted a madman, I would give them one. I kissed all the girls and began turning up at people's homes at mealtimes. More often than not, I ended up at my Rainbow's home, because she had never doubted that love was safe and sound. Mother was fully aware that I was still singing. And so was Hizam. He took me aside one day and showed me his knife: "You kiss my

daughter one more time and I will kill you. I'm not
crazy, and the only crazy thing about you is that you're
song crazy. You can make fools of all of them for all I
care. But not of me, not in my house."

I lived my madness to the hilt and went around
telling people all the things the old woman told me. No
one dared to cross me. Through it all, I never stopped
being a model student, top of my class, all the teachers
praising me to the skies. Father was both jealous and
proud of me, and Mother kept pushing me to sing. In
the end, the villagers were to pay dearly for their heated
imaginings. No one, not the woman who wanted me to
remain forever small so that she could go on kissing me,
not even my Rainbow, was spared.

When the old woman died, we learned she had entrusted Hizam with her will. One Friday afternoon,
after Friday prayer, the village gathered to hear Hizam
deliver the following brief message: "I leave all my
lands to the one who avenged me, the village bard and
poet." The sadness in Hizam's voice was hard to miss.
He had done everything in his power to convince the
old woman to sell him her lands before she died. Turning to me, he said:

"My wealth, when all is said and done, didn't amount
to much compared to your singing."

The village took me back into its fold, but soon afterward I was forced to leave it despite myself. I went off
to become the journalist of my father's and teachers'

dreams, and in an act of pure folly, I left my Rainbow behind. The village had already seen a few of its young men make the move to the capital. All of them worked in security at the main hospital and had been brought on board thanks to the good graces of the fellow villager who ran the department, a very able man whose position had brought him in contact with all the most powerful people in the country. In a way, he was a kind of village head—but in the city.

These new city boys ate all their meals at the hospital and, as a result, never spent a penny of their earnings. Hizam and the rest of the village folk had never in their lives come across such words as *hospital, capital, police—* and *salary* was the newest one of all. The hospital became a kind of golden dream for the villagers. It was a kind of heaven on earth; after all, their boys were not only housed, clothed, and fed at no cost whatever to themselves, they were also given a salary, money they barely touched until it was time to go home to the village. Many fathers were eager to send their sons to this hospital that had become a kind of free hotel. Still, work there could not always be guaranteed, and there were those who were turned away and ended up in the village a few months later, empty-handed.

Then one afternoon, the head of hospital security came to visit. The whole village turned up, drawn, no doubt, by the whiff of the capital and money to burn, to greet this symbol of success. The precious task of

unloading his car of its cargo of bags and boxes fell only
to his family members and those closest to him. He was
given the welcome he was entitled to, and then we all
followed him into his house.

The man, who would thereafter be known as the
Capital, told us his news as custom requires even after a
single morning's absence. He then turned to the fathers
of the young men on his staff and told them their police
officer sons had sent them money, lots of money, and
gifts, thereby setting off a twinge of envy throughout
the room.

The Capital stood up. He had a fat belly and a splayed
way of walking. His feet were hidden—sheathed in the
first pair of socks the village had ever laid eyes on—and
he didn't wear a belt! No one was more mortified than
Hizam, who, from that moment on, could only bring
himself either to stare at the ceiling or gaze at his knife.
The Capital's brothers carried several cardboard boxes
into the room—new clothes for everyone in the village.
In no time, we were all wearing our new outfits on top
of our everyday clothing, imposing the capital on the
village, so to speak. We stayed in that attire for two
whole days—two unforgettable days. In the end, we de-
sisted because the month of Ramadan was just around
the corner, and we wanted to save our new clothes for
the holiday.

At night, the men talked about the government,
about the capital and its riches, while Hizam beseeched

God to grant a long life to our founding monarch, never mind the fact, never really accepted by Hizam, that the man had been dead for decades. The family of the Capital celebrated his homecoming in a style befitting such a man. Never before had we tasted tea and coffee laced with cardamom. The Capital had bought his father a mattress—another first in the village—and a blanket. He asked his father to test it out right there in the middle of the sitting room with all the guests looking on. Why not take a few days off, he urged, rest a while, to hell with the fields. He begged his old father to live like a king.

On the next night, we were again summoned, for dinner this time. Ten sheep, slaughtered for the occasion, were carried in on ten separate platters especially purchased in the capital. We finally tasted that famous so-called rice of which we had only dreamed. They served us *kapsa,* a dish made of rice and lamb. Usually, the choice pieces of meat were parceled out among the village dignitaries, and the rest of us, especially the children, were sometimes left with nothing but the aroma. But this *kapsa* was a minor revolution: we all ate at the same time as the grown-ups and the leftovers were sent along to be divided among the women and girls who had stayed at home.

Every now and again, our indefatigable host would pause in his stories about civilized life in the capital to produce a cigarette, which he would light before our very eyes. Now, nobody in the village smoked. Even the activity was referred to as drinking, not smoking, a cigarette. We only knew of a handful of nomads and shepherds who smoked on the sly and secretly bought their tobacco from the old neighbor who had a few tobacco plants growing on her roof terrace. The best time to pass unseen was during the Friday noon prayer, a ritual the smokers did not observe with the rest of the village. As a result, we considered all smokers a personal affront.

The moment he lit up, the traveler began to lose credibility in our eyes, but this was a minor breach compared to the shock of his gold tooth. We began to wonder if he only smiled to display it. A strange and alien odor seeped into the house. We had never smelled anything so fetid in the village. Hizam even swore that he had been forced to hold his nose for the first time in his life.

The Capital stayed behind with his cigarettes and tooth of gold as the men went off to ready themselves for dancing. Except for Hizam—he never danced. Everyone in the village was sure it was because he didn't know how to. But he really didn't like dancing of any kind. He claimed it was dangerous, at times even deadly for those with a weak constitution. Dancers were lightweights in every sense of the word, but not tonight. Tonight, the joy that had been elicited by the traveler's arrival gave way to defiance, defiance against him and the civilized life of which he spoke. The village was sad, wounded. Later, we heard that even the Capital's father had wept.

The Memory of Water

Time and again, the village would run out of water. And despite the extravagant number of wells our ancestors had seen fit to dig, we were often caught short when it came time to irrigate the fields. Once, with the wheat harvest just weeks away and only one small section of his field irrigated, I saw Hizam strip down to almost nothing and reach down with both hands to lift large clumps of earth, which he then flung at his head and body as if to turn himself into a parched plant on which God would take pity. He then looked up and called on the sky to be his witness and said: "You alone can bring the rains. And believe me, I would if I were you. So, do it!" After that, he went over to his bull and stood still as a post. A few minutes elapsed and then rain started to fall from the sky, from the mountains, and from the valleys. A number of us could have attested to what we had seen with our very own eyes, but only the word of circumcised men counted for anything in the village. Who was going to listen to small fry like us who still wore their hair like boys? Shaven, except for a tuft sprouting out of the crown and a band of close-cropped hair encircling the head like a belt from which long, uncut locks dangled over our ears. "For people to put any stock in what you have to say," Father announced one day, "first, we'll have to cut your hair. Don't worry, you won't be the only one. There are about ten of you, and arrangements have already been made for tomorrow morning." Father cut my hair. Sister didn't sing, and sleep came to no one that night. Father set out at first light to fetch the circumcision master, but they must have missed one another because the man turned up first and alone. I was waiting with Mother and my maternal uncle.

I was circumcised in the old way, but without festivities. We were all very young, and our fathers, anticipating that many of us would cry or even faint, decided we would be better off in the privacy of our own homes. Much had changed since the coming of the school, and our parents were letting many of the traditions fall by the wayside. Only our mothers stood their ground and set about hastily giving the houses a fresh coat of paint, as had been the custom for generations.

While I stood there reciting verses about my genealogy, pain must have pushed me overboard and I cursed the lineage of the circumcision master, but the man remained nonplussed. After finishing the job, he kissed me, and just before leaving, he said I could cry when I got safely home, which is exactly what I did. But when I heard what my paternal uncle had in mind, my crying rose to new heights. The master, this uncle claimed, had stinted, missed a couple of stubborn shreds. With my circumcised cousins to assist him by holding down my legs, he began cutting away at what he called the scraps of shame. I don't know what would have happened if Father hadn't walked in with tears of pride and joy in his eyes to put a stop to it all. Mother had already gathered the fig leaves and prepared the rock powder that would speed my healing.

A couple of days later, Hizam gave me a belt and a knife: "Take these, you're a man now. This is a sacred moment, one you must never betray. Never forget, women are man's greatest handicap. From now on, you love only your fields, you sing only to your fields."

Even though we had been circumcised in the old way, we didn't enjoy any of the traditional festivities that had always been part of circumcision: even my pretty cousin was a married woman now. My Rainbow was the only one who brought a ray of light into the new austerity the school had imposed on my village. She sent me one of her belts. It was impregnated with her smell, and I have kept it to this day, along with one that was my mother's.

Before our circumcisions, we were no more than children to the women, and the men saw us as something still very much in the rough. Circumcision marked our real initiation into life. Hizam said we had passed both exams with flying colors—the sixth-grade one and the manhood one. This double victory was the absolute go-ahead we needed to leave the village and return to the city where we had obtained our birth certificates and would now attend high school. But this time we were going for three whole years, and our fathers weren't coming with us.

Leaving the village was a kind of death for me. As I think back on it, it was water that helped assuage my pain and fear. Yes, water was my talisman. Our village had, after all, been founded on water; its memory, its history, its conflicts, its secrets, or its soul, as Hizam used to say, inhered in water. I went around the village with my eyes closed, moving from well to well, drinking and bathing in every single one. I loved my village, knew it inside and out—every animal and every tree, every work tool, the feel of its days and of its nights, the familiar smells of people and of rain, the true hour for everything.

Hizam insisted I look at every single document that had anything to do with the village and passed the entirety of his knowledge on to me so that I would be ready to take his place when the time came. He showed me the two holes where the sun never fails to fall, once in summer for the sowing of wheat and barley and once in winter for corn and winter grain. Then he showed me the stars, all of them. And as he spoke, a feeling came over me that he was touching them. Stars, like us, marry, he said. The other village sage believed they were free to love where they chose—like the trees and the rocks and the sand, like water, like wind. And knowledge in its entirety, the life force itself, rested on this principle. Our village was divided between those who followed him and those who followed Hizam.

The only time the two of them had been seen together was when they went to welcome a third man who had just returned from Sweden, where he had taken his daughter for treatment at the government's expense. We immediately took to calling him the Swede. (Before his Swedish sojourn, everyone called him Pair of Peckers. He had the old woman who lived next door to thank for that.) The Swede had us all in a fever of excitement with his tales of distant wonders: the Northern women, the sun that never sets, the bicycles, the televisions, the telephones, and the cars. But especially the Swedish women. We couldn't hear enough about their thighs, their eyes, their hair. The older men in the village visited the Swede for weeks on end, until they had wrung the river dry. Apparently, one of the old-timers even said: "Good thing you were twice endowed!" and then went on to claim he was the only one in the village who really lived in the Swedish way because he had three wives and the youngest one even looked like a Swede. But the imam put a quick stop to all that and advised him to keep whatever went on between him and his wives to himself. Hizam couldn't have agreed more.

Thanks to the Swede we became aware of another

world, a world outside the village from which he had managed to return in one piece, even if he had trimmed his beard somewhat. His daughter also did her part, telling the women all about Sweden. She had come back with underwear and a watch. Her father also wore one, and whenever we ran into him, we'd ask him the time, even though we were never entirely sure what we were asking.

The Swedish phase lasted several weeks and helped ready the village emotionally for our impending departure to the city.

Father was suffering from a hernia that kept growing and growing. Treatment for his condition could only be had in the capital, at the hospital that in some sense belonged to the village. But Father didn't have enough money for either his journey or mine. Three friends to whom I will remain eternally grateful lent him the money he needed. He gave me half and bought me a new white outfit, notebooks, ink, a suitcase, and a few bunches of dates out of the other half. He also left some money for Mother and Sister. I'm not sure how much he was left with for himself in the end.

Hizam hosted us on the eve of our departure. He produced some underwear and gave a pair to his son and one to me and told us: "Protect your peckers and your money. It's your honor and ours that is at stake. And if I hear you've strayed in any way, I'll come in person to bring you back home." Afterward, we went and called on every family in the village. Mothers kissed us on the lips, and we kissed the fathers on their foreheads. The day we left was a dark day for the village. There was mourning in every house on the day we left.

The City of Clouds

We were in the car, on our way to the city, when my friend showed me the money his father had given him. Without letting on to the other boys, we decided to lump our money together. At journey's end, the older boys, who had already spent an entire year in the city, were expecting us. I went to unpack and found the ink had spilled all over the dream outfit Father had bought me. I was devastated. Then, one of the older boys told me about a magic detergent. We set out in search of it right away and couldn't stop marveling at how it made the ink stains disappear. The boy who knew about these things told us it was a Swedish product, and Sweden again became the main topic of our conversations.

Very soon after we settled in, I realized that there was even more poetry in this city than there had been in the village. I was sure that city dwellers were really village poets who preferred singing to tilling. They danced the nights away, and every last one of them, the older boys included, was in love. The large house we rented was a stone's throw from the hospital—from the Pakistani nurses, to be precise.

I decided to look after my friend, whose money didn't even cover his share of the rent. He took to saying I was his true father. Each one of us had been supplied with a sack of flour and some butter and honey. We started every day by baking our own pan bread and got every morning off to a miserable start because the stuff we turned out was nothing like the bread our mothers had baked in the village.

At school, the city boys bought themselves sandwiches and fruit juices. We'd sit in the sun and try to fool hunger by humming behind closed mouths as Mother had done so often. When school let out, we rushed home to cook up our daily pot of rice. In the evening, we baked more bread and brewed very sweet tea to ease it down. And it was like this every day of the week except for Friday, blissful Fridays, when we bought sesame loaves from the store.

Every morning we awoke with renewed energy to gaze on the beautiful nurses next door, and every afternoon we tried to satiate our famished stomachs with the wonderful smells emerging from the hospital kitchen. This was our daily regimen, a torment we gladly endured. Actually, we considered ourselves privileged, even fortunate, and couldn't help wondering why more people didn't choose to live near the hospital.

Cities are invariably built in places where there is

a treasure underground, Hizam had told me one day. People were drawn to them from everywhere by the promise of gold. In time, tired of searching, they would give up and calm would be restored. Then one fine day they would wake up and completely forget a treasure had ever existed. The hospital, as I saw it, stood for such a treasure, but there was a high wall surrounding it and guards watching over it, and the only thing flowing out of there was the smell of food.

When we were done with our special Friday breakfast, we would set off to bathe and wash our clothing. For this, we walked past the city limits until we reached the outlying villages so achingly reminiscent of ours, surrounded by fields where life could be snatched with tooth and claw from time and sun and rain. Everyone from the village, regardless of sex or age, bore a cut or a scar of some kind. From Hizam, we had learned to piss on the cuts on our feet before plastering them with earth, which we let dry. The knives we carried everywhere were more often used to dig out thorns that had lodged themselves in our feet than to fend off enemies or slaughter sheep. It was only after I had lived in the city for a while that I came to realize I had nails. They never had much of a chance to grow before because of all the work we did using our hands as tools.

We lived in far greater proximity to the sun in the city than we had ever been in the village. Our skin, as a result, was considerably drier. Also, we rarely, if ever, had any milk or butter, whereas in the village we could drink our fill of milk and slather ourselves with butter. In the village, we shone. But in the city, we took on a dun earthen color. Still, most of the time, we lived in the clouds. People here spoke of clouds much as people at home spoke of fields. We all knew our clouds inside out and even arranged to meet under this or that cloud— every now and then, animals would stray and wander into the wrong cloud. That's what happened when a herd of so-called Egyptian goats, their teats bursting with milk, came into our lives. The leader of our little gang thrilled us by suggesting we milk them by drawing just a little milk from each one. We all agreed this was a capital idea. We lured the goats with scraps of bread, and for the first time since we had set foot in the city, we all drank milky tea that day. The goats seemed to like our bread almost as much as we liked their milk, and we started milking them daily, always taking care not to overdo it so that the man who owned them wouldn't notice a thing.

We were beginning to get back some of our old village color when another tenant in the house, a student who was as foreign to these parts as we were, tipped off the owner to our little racket. The owner, it turned out, had purchased the goats so that his elderly parents with their frail appetites could at least have milk during the Ramadan fast, and he as much as said he would turn a blind eye, if we agreed to give the milking a rest until the holy month was behind us.

Our neighbor, the tattler, eventually turned up one day to convey his Ramadan wishes. He lived alone in a windowless and smelly room: unlike the rest of us, who had condemned them as absolutely off limits from the moment we saw them, he used the toilets. We still did our business in the village way. The landlord's daughter had complained to my friends that the little one (meaning me) did it wherever he pleased. My friends were quick to deny this and defend me as a true cat when it came to answering the call of nature. I was deeply hurt by the accusation because I felt it as a blow to the way Mother had raised me and to our village code of cleanliness. Also, the girls, who were very beautiful, obviously considered me no more than a child despite the fact I had been circumcised. I was in love with the youngest one and her mother was onto me. And even her kind words weren't much help at all.

I would have liked for us to move, but we didn't even have enough money to pay the rent. I was penniless; the money Father had given me was long gone. We had received only one sack of flour from my friend's father and nothing from Mother because she had nothing to send and Father was still laid up in the capital undergoing treatment.

A cousin to whom I was closely related lived in a

nearby town. He was one of the richest men in the area at the time. The sack of wheat that was to blame for Father's hernia had been destined for him. Father had, in fact, warned me never to rely on this particular cousin, but what could I do? Even after I went to the trouble and expense of taking a taxi to reach his house, my cousin just stood there, swearing up and down on the Qur'an that he had no ready cash, and then he asked one of his taxi driver friends to drive me home free of charge. Never had I felt so humiliated, and I made sure the driver knew I would pay him for the fare as soon as I had the means.

I came home empty-handed and wept in front of the other boys. After I told them the whole sorry story, the older boys wanted a word in private. I took heart, thinking they had come up with a solution to my problems, and was completely bewildered to hear them broach a completely different matter. A neighbor, it seemed, had approached the oldest boy and accused me of theft. I had purportedly stolen a cassette player and taken it to my cousin's house for safekeeping. My head was immediately full of thoughts of my mother and father, my village. I wanted to die there and then. I wanted the earth to open up and swallow me whole. I remembered my mother's parting words to me. "Don't forget God," she said. Well, where was he? I certainly needed him now. I prayed hard for a miracle and never breathed a word about it to the others.

No one ate dinner that evening. Who had the heart to eat? We were all in the same boat. The older boys paced round and round in circles. The tears I wept were hotter than the sun, my eyesight blurry from so much crying. My friend sat next to me blubbering away as if he was the one who had been accused. He was crying so hard I couldn't even hear myself sob. Anyway, to make a long story short, we were all in a sea of tears by the time the landlord arrived. He wanted to speak to the older boys, but we insisted we all had to hear what he had to say. My accuser had suffered a fit, a seizure had paralyzed his limbs, and the landlord was here on his behalf to apologize and ask for my forgiveness. The true guilty party, it turned out, was none other than the accuser's own son. I came to my senses in a flash; my parents, my village, my friends rushed to fill my thoughts. The dark shadows that had engulfed me began to lift, but forgiveness was beyond me. How could I forgive? I already had a vision of myself with my right hand chopped off or locked up in prison for an eternity, now that Islamic law was replacing all tribal laws. I knew how easily one could be sentenced, given the brisk traffic in false testimonies. One could always find people who were willing to take the serious risk of being caught lying by the judge. But worst of all, this incident could have tarnished all the hopes my village had placed in me. My triumphs at school had prevailed over my lapses as a tribesman. I was neither brave nor valiant, hardly the

warrior longed after by village tradition. I was quite the
opposite, in fact. I was often weepy and even suffered
from dizzy spells. But my performance at school had
turned me into a symbol, and all the village fathers
loved me and praised me at their gatherings. Not to
mention all the people who, in keeping with village custom, had named their children after me. I was my father's pride and joy. Wherever he went, people wanted
to speak to him of me, and there wasn't one among his
friends who didn't wish he too had been blessed with
such a son. My success at school had become the supreme value. And even though it had been easy for me
to come by, I had, as a result, become a symbol for my
whole tribe.

My friends and I took a solemn vow never to divulge
a word about all the things that transpired on that fate-
ful day. They were to be buried and forgotten, and I am
sure I am the first to break our pact.

We had all followed Hizam's advice to the letter;
some of us even bathed fully clothed and all of us still
had our peckers. We tried our best to peek at the nurses
as surreptitiously as possible. And as for money, life in
the city without it was out of the question; at the very
least, we needed the bare minimum to cover the cost of
rice and rent.

Those days were the saddest of my life. I had no
news of Father. And the news from Mother wasn't exactly reassuring. Ramadan was coming around, and I

had no choice but to stand in for Father and see our family well provided for during the upcoming holiday. I decided to go see another one of my city cousins, even though he had never taken the trouble to show his face, to apprise him of my situation and ask for his help. He was the one who told me the news from Father was not very encouraging. He also offered to vouch for me with the merchant, who turned out to be that sometime villager who had sold everything, even his share of wind.

We arrived at the shop to find it full of men who had left the village many years before. They all knew Father because he had helped them out back in the days when they were poor village dwellers. While my cousin conferred with the merchant about my dire circumstances, the men praised Father's generosity and loyalty. They could have saved their breath, for all the good it did. The merchant was not impressed, and when I tried to put my case before him, he was ready for me.

"I'm very fond of your father, my boy, but who's to say if he'll ever come back, and this gentleman's word just isn't enough to go on. Wait until you receive your scholarship money from the government, as I am sure you will at the end of the year, and then you can come back on your own terms, buy whatever you like, and take your father's place. In the meantime, however, you should be paying more attention to your studies. Nothing good can come of incurring debts at your age. You're such a tiny thing, I can barely make you out. I know your mother will not be happy when she hears the condition you're in. You look like something that crawled out of a grave."

Ordinarily, I would have dissolved into tears, but this time, his roughshod treatment coupled with the good holiday wishes he was sending my mother drove me to fury. I reached for every sack of coffee, cardamom, rice, and tea I could get my hands on and slit them from top to bottom, spilling their contents all over the floor. Then I flew out of there with the wind at my heels and went to tell my friends what had happened. We put on our belts and knives and went back to settle the score. The merchant, who was cleaning up the mess while cursing the village and the tribe, fell silent when he saw us coming.

But it was his lucky day. The owner of the neighboring store happened to be a man who knew our village; he knew our fathers and our history and the way our village had fought off the Turks, and he intervened in the nick of time by proposing himself as our supplier. We could help ourselves to anything we needed and pay him when we received our scholarship money at the end of the year. He would keep a record of all our purchases and set an individual credit limit for each one of us. But first, we had to agree to dine with him one evening. I think he wanted to pay his respects to our village and teach all those city people a lesson. The meal he served us was the stuff of dreams: salads, *kapsa*, desserts.

Our host had arranged things so that we would be left alone to enjoy the meal in peace—yet another sign of his generosity. But despite being ravenous, we abided by tribal etiquette and limited ourselves to a small taste of the dishes that were set before us, and in keeping with village custom, we all rose as a man when the meal came to an end. When our host noticed that we had barely touched the food, he confided in us that he had always wished to belong to our tribe. And then he quoted the famous lines spoken by the Prophet: "We are of those who eat only when hungry and never eat to their hunger's satisfaction." The luxurious meal had taken us a bit by surprise, but the real eye-opener was the water flowing hot and cold from separate taps and the fancy soaps and all the other wonderful things within our reach. When we had finished our meal, our host perfumed our hands and clothing. And even though Hizam had taught us perfume was only for women, we put off washing those clothes until every trace of scent had vanished.

When the evening drew to a close, he made us a gift of an alarm clock, which only my friend knew how to operate properly. We had never had watches or radios or electricity or gas or toothbrushes or books—with the exception of schoolbooks—or magazines or newspapers, but we knew how to sing.

The Time of Djinns

Ramadan was approaching. Our prayers now included the *tarawih,* a special prayer that is very long and performed only during this sacred month. These lengthy sessions at the mosque provided a perfect opportunity for a handful of foreign students to go around stealing the shoes of the faithful. And even though we all knew we could end up losing a hand in the process, it didn't take us long to cave in to temptation and follow their lead.

I had always been the best student, the one with the highest grades, until the day my teacher noticed his shoes on my feet. As expected, he was wearing mine. I cried and blathered something about an honest mistake. I gave him his shoes, he gave me mine, and then followed them up with my first bad grade. But even such a close call didn't stop me from later stealing the softest, most exquisite shoes in the city to make a gift of them to my mother.

One morning, we paid a visit to our kind purveyor and stocked up on coffee, sugar, tea, and cardamom. We wanted to make the most of the ride we had secured in a car that was headed in the general direction of the village, so we left behind the city that had hardened us and went home, proud to be returning with laden arms. This was the first time we felt like grown-ups, like the men who worked in the capital whom we so wanted to emulate. The smell of the village air was coming back to us, and with it the eyes and smiles and joy of all those we would soon be seeing. The separation had been harsh.

The driver dropped us off some twenty kilometers from the village, and we covered the remaining distance on foot. It was almost the end of Ramadan and the sun was already setting, and we were hungry and thirsty because naturally we had been fasting since sunrise. We took off our shoes so as not to ruin them and began to walk in earnest. It was late night by the time we reached the village, but, as expected, all the men, women, and children were waiting for us, everyone except for Father. The other fathers did their best to make up for his being away and welcomed me as they would their own sons, but this didn't stop me from tearing up when Mother held me in her arms.

Mother now treated me as the man of the house. She was very distant. I showed her the things I brought back, and she went to the kitchen and brewed me some coffee. Her words were wet with tears. My-Sister-My-Memory found me handsome and told me all the girls had been impatient for us to come home. She also told me Father wouldn't be home for the holiday. We ate our dinner in silence, not even daring to exchange a look. The house began to feel emptier and emptier. Heavy and cold. I opened the window onto the enormous night. All I wanted was to breathe in my father's smell, to rub his tired feet. We were there like three orphans, and even my homecoming wasn't enough to distract us from the fact that the true man in our lives was missing.

In the night, I once again became my mother's son. She made me sleep where Father usually slept and placed his walking stick and knife by my side. I tried with all my might to summon up the smell of the absent man. And even though it was cold, I kept the window slightly ajar the way he always liked it. By morning, someone had closed it.

Father was usually the one who called the village to prayer, but the voice we heard that morning was someone else's. I was awakened by his absence. We all gathered at the mosque for the dawn prayer. I went alone, and after the prayer, the imam asked me to stay. Father was gravely ill. His operation had not been successful. But he was alive. The imam assured me of it over and over again when he saw how I was weeping.

But even the imam's reassuring words could not alleviate my anxious heart, and I had no way of going to my father. Whenever I saw Hizam, he'd say the same thing: "I was younger than you are now when I lost my father." It didn't mean that he wasn't just as sad as I was.

One evening, Mother told me the story of a black slave who lost his son. The master ordered the slave back to irrigate the fields as soon as they had finished burying his boy. He didn't even give the man a chance to gather his thoughts and feelings by the child's graveside. The slave did not protest and walked toward the field singing:

> Oh, raven!
> Dark raven!
> Fruit I buried deep in the ground.
> Fruit of my heart.
> You were my fruit, my soul,
> and who can bury the soul?
> Oh, night dark fruit.
> Would they had buried my eyes.
> Oh, night dark fruit.
> Would they had buried me.

When the master heard the slave singing, he called him to his side and said, "You know you have no right to sing."

"I know, you've told me so before, but I was simply weeping."

"No, you were singing, and you taught me freedom."

"Everyone is free in his own way," the slave answered.

"Say I were to trade you a field for a song?"

"Then, I," said the slave, "would be your master."

"Everyone is free in his own way," the master replied.

The night before I was to leave, my mother told me another story. A long time ago, djinns outnumbered human beings a hundred times over. They were everywhere and could disguise themselves as trees and rocks and flowers and turn themselves into water and birds and animals. They were everywhere one looked or listened or walked or loved, in every place one spoke or dressed or ate. And folly was their weapon of choice. If you so much as offended them, even slightly, even unwittingly, then folly would quickly follow. Invoking God's name was the only recourse people had before embarking on any activity, especially eating. Those who neglected to invoke God before a meal may have been under the impression they were eating, but actually the djinns made off with most of the food. "Look around you," Mother used to say, "and you'll see that the world is divided into wholesome and hearty souls who invoke the name of God and their skinny, starved, and diseased counterparts who forget. And the children of those who invoke God's name before lovemaking are healthy, intelligent, and polite, while the other ones are their exact opposite. And that's how it is for everything. Djinns inhabit nature, they are nature itself. Let me tell you what happened to one of my cousins. My family used to grow grapes back then, and this particular cousin was in charge of keeping the monkeys and other wild animals out of the vineyard. One night, he heard a noise deep inside the arbor, and thinking nothing of it, he fired his gun in its general direction. In no time, the entire valley was overrun by djinns, all of them dressed in green, the women wearing their long hair down. The most radiant of these longhaired beauties began to sing a song of death, a lament for the djinn prince who was dying of a bullet wound:

> You, murderer of our princely son.
> You've killed our heart and murdered our soul.
> A pox on your crops,
> You, killer of our dream.
> May they fail in summer
> and again in winter.

"The djinns started moving toward the place where my cousin lay hiding, but he spoke the magic words and was saved from the jaws of death.

"In the old days, human beings could see the djinns clear as day. Human and djinn lived side by side. Those were the days when water knew all our thoughts and feelings. And secrets were as unthinkable as life without water. Djinns and human beings only needed words for their songs, and their words bristled with colors. Things could have remained that way forever, if a human man had not fallen in love with one of their daughters. The lovers had everyone's blessing to marry, but only on one condition. The human man had to promise to never, ever remark on what a shame it was for such a beautiful creature to have the hooves of a goat instead of human feet. Unfortunately, the man was not equal to such love. The bride's clan was banished from the great tribe of the djinns. They were exiled into eternal darkness and their skin turned dark. In the end, they were punished twice over, excluded by both djinns and human beings. The slave in the story belonged to this tribe, a tribe of landless people who were dispersed and went into service for others, like the *Tarafs* with us."

Mother's story was cut short by a bat that fell winded at our feet. There were many in the house. They nested in ceilings and under stairs, especially on the landing where the animals slept and where there was hardly any light to speak of. This one had apparently gone astray. Mother picked up the creature and stroked it as tenderly and respectfully as she would her own child. She fetched butter and rubbed it all over her hands and lost herself in a strange ceremony. She seemed to be counting every hair on that bat's body. Her gestures were accompanied by prayers and strange words I had never heard before. I've always suspected my mother of secretly holding on to beliefs that had nothing to do with Islam. Without taking her eyes off the bat, she asked me to light the fire and open every window in the house. I expect it was a ruse to be left alone.

My sister appeared, her eyes heavy with sleep. "Here's another bat," I said to Mother. I began to stroke her as Mother was stroking the bat, and my sister was soon coaxed back to sleep. At dawn, the bat opened its eyes and began to stir. And Mother was her old self again.

"We saved it!" she cried. "Now, it can go to Heaven."

"Heaven? Isn't Heaven for human beings?"

"This bat is the tormented soul of one of your ancestors. And God granted it one last chance to come among the living to cleanse itself of sin. I made a vow and took all the sins upon myself, even those I didn't entirely understand. But look, you saw for yourself, it just flew away. And this time, it's going straight to Heaven."

"But what about you? You may have saved a soul, but what about when you stand alone before God, burdened with someone else's sins as well as your own? I have no desire to meet you as a bat someday!"

"You're mistaken, son. God picked me to save this soul, and saving one soul, in God's eyes, is tantamount to saving all humanity. I have been blessed with splendid luck, a chance to save my soul from Hell. It was sublime, like witnessing the Night of Destiny. Your mother, my son, is Heaven-bound."

This was hardly news to me. I always knew Mother was destined straight for Heaven. My mother—always the last to eat and often pretending she had already eaten when there wasn't enough to go around. She *was* Heaven, as far as I was concerned. But if I ever said this to her, she would remind me of the man who had devoted his life entirely to God. On the day he died, God presented him with a choice. He could choose to be judged by his actions or by the will of God. He chose the first and went straight to Hell. As he was plummeting, the man turned one last time to God and cried out, "By your will! Your will!" And God sent him to Heaven. Basically, God wants us to serve both Heaven and ourselves. This is how life takes on meaning.

I had always seen my mother as a poem, a poem of eternal renewal. That night, I understood that my mother was a human being like any other. I touched her feet and kissed them. They looked slightly swollen. Mother, I thought, can only look forward to an ordinary life now, a life of illness, weariness, petty worries, and old age. A run-of-the-mill kind of life.

Mother hardly ever sang anymore, and Father was ill and far away. Sister spent her days sleeping or pretending to. It suddenly hit me that ours was a sick house. A house without music or poetry is a terrifying place. For me, the shock was profound. I felt at a loss and went looking for Hizam to ask for his help. He took one look at my face and took me down into the cellar where he kept his treasure and where no one, he swore to me, had ever set foot. The place was so dark I couldn't see a thing. He came straight to the point and asked me how much money I needed.

"Forty rials," I answered.

"This treasure is my life's work," he said, "the life of my entire family. This wealth was amassed by the labor of several generations. I don't have forty rials, and I wouldn't even give you twenty."

"Fifteen?"

"No."

"So, ten then?"

"Get the hell out of here!"

"How? I can't see a thing down here."

"Well, you should've thought of that before coming down. Do you have any idea what ten rials means to a man like me?" he asked, as he handed the money over. "Year after year of work and travel. I'll be dead and in my grave by the time you'll be able to pay me back."

"At the end of the year, I'll pay you from my scholarship money. The government gives us one hundred rials a month."

"One hundred rials! What! Either they're lunatics or their money is no better than dust. This ten rials I am giving you is equal to ten men. Do you understand? Sure, you can give it back to me at the end of the year, but I want you to know its value won't be the same. This is my proud earnings. In my day, we didn't have a government, and anyway, I would never allow myself to be bought like that. I don't like easy money."

"But you yourself used to say we were all sons of the government. And it's the same government that gives us the money. And ten of their rials still buys the same amount of coffee as ten of yours."

"You understand nothing. This money is dear, very dear money. It comes at a terribly high price. It has moral weight, my son. But why does the government give you a hundred rials a month if you already lack for nothing, when you're already clothed and shod and sheltered from sun and inclement weather without so much as lifting a finger? This government is dishonest."

"We're being trained to become engineers and doctors and pilots and journalists and other things."

"Exactly, it's those other things I'm worried about."

"You don't have to worry about me, Hizam."

"Who says I'm worried about you? I'm worried about this village that you're all going to leave behind someday."

"I know you are giving me part of yourself by giving me this ten rials. And I am thankful, I thank you from the bottom of my heart. But you're really lending this money to my father."

"True, but I want *you* to pay me back."

I went home and gave Mother half the money. She thanked me with a wink. The villagers gathered to see us off. The car took off in a cloud of dust and tears. After it dropped us off in the city, the older boys continued toward the capital in search of work and a better life. We felt like orphans without them, but nothing could be done about it. Before we knew it, we were back in our daily round of poverty, humiliation, and hunger, living in a small city that mercifully still could sing.

I undid my small suitcase and was surprised to find the stolen shoes sitting on top. I immediately understood that although Mother had accepted the gift, she could not accept the theft, and I took them back straightaway. The imam was there. I wanted to hide my face for shame. And while he recited verses from the Qur'an, I put the shoes back in their rightful place and never set foot in that mosque again.

The Sheep and the Writer

With the older boys off making a living in the capital, I became a kind of father to the others. "A father without money," says the proverb, "is like a firearm without ammunition." And nowhere was this truer than in the city. It hardly seemed to matter that with the older boys gone we now had no one to count on but ourselves; our neighbors still saw us as children. In an effort to redress this impression, we wore our belts and knives everywhere and only took them off when we had to go to school. We flaunted the name of our village and wrote it on the walls of the house, and, as a further assertion of our independence, we stopped attending the neighborhood mosque. We preferred to pray by ourselves, with only one another for company. We fell in with this way of life until the day one of the boys came home stripped of his belt and knife. A humiliation of this kind was tantamount to social death. At least that's how he saw it—when he was screaming and crying and scratching his face, and his shame was also ours.

A man who lived in the neighborhood had caught

him talking to his one and only daughter, a girl who
bore the name of the city where we all lived. This man
had also seen fit to name his house Egypt, because Egypt
is the mother of the universe, after all. He had a reputation of fearing nothing and no one, except for his wife,
who was every woman's bane because she knew all the
neighborhood secrets. I took one of the boys along, a
very handsome one, and we went to pay her a call. Her
husband went out of his way to pretend he hadn't noticed us and sat silent as a post throughout our visit.
It didn't take me long to see him as another one who
was his wife's wife. This kind of matter was customarily
handled by tribal heads, but the woman who sat before
us seemed to have all the necessary qualities to bring
things to a good end. We had come for the belt and knife
and wanted them returned to their rightful owner.

She began by apologizing for her husband's offense,
and then, refusing to take no for an answer, she promised to hand over our belongings at the dinner she was
inviting us to share with her later that evening. Her husband had still not made a peep. Later, when the food
was set out before us on the table, my friend told our
hostess, who was devouring him with her eyes:

"The belt and knife have to be returned before we
can touch this food, my lady."

She fetched the belt and knife and placed them into
his hands with a look only city women can muster. Her
husband chose that moment to leave, telling her to take

good care of the children—he meant us. His departure didn't seem to perturb her in the least. He was in the habit of using company as an excuse to leave the house, or so she said.

Now that our honor had been restored, we were ready to tuck into the food. And I must say we ate very well. When it came time for us to leave, she asked the handsome boy to stay behind and help her write a letter to her son, who was away making a living in the capital. It was very late when he came home that night. And from that moment on, he became the official neighborhood scribe. All the women wanted him to write letters for them, even the ones who didn't have sons in the capital, and afterward, he always came home with a pot of rice and meat. He shared everything with us—except the writing.

The imam turned up one day with the following proposition: we could all move into his house free of charge as long as we agreed to pray at the mosque like everyone else. I asked the handsome one if he had been writing letters for the imam's wife as well, but not only was the imam a widower who had no sons in the capital, he was also a neighborhood scribe himself.

"Do you and the imam practice the same kind of writing?" I wanted to know.

"Only God knows. To each man his qualities and his quill."

All women were poets, according to my friend, and

it wasn't easy to transcribe their feelings simply by writing. At any rate, none of us were complaining; we were happy for the free food and lodging. Sometimes he would even take my clothing and bring it back laundered and ironed. Practice must have done wonders for my friend's style, because before long his reputation had spread throughout the city. He was very busy moving from one neighborhood to the next, even skipping school sometimes.

One day, while he was off on his rounds, his father showed up. I told him his son was away in Egypt. One of the other boys backed me up on this, confounding matters even further by adding that he went to Egypt almost every day and always came back with a pot of rice and meat. We hadn't finished having our bit of fun with the man when his son walked in, steaming pot in hand.

"I'd give anything to see this Egypt," his father said.

"Let's eat first, and then we can all go there for coffee."

"How in heaven's name do you do it?"

"You'll see for yourself soon enough."

The imam and other neighborhood dignitaries came by to greet our visitor and welcome him to the city. The imam complimented him on having taught his son to write so well.

"I can neither read nor write. I barely know how to pray," the man said. "But give me a field, and I'll show you a thing or two about tilling the land. Ask any one of the boys, they'll tell you."

He was right. His fields were admired by everyone in the village in much the same way people admire the works of great masters nowadays. The man made it clear he had never undertaken a single activity in his life without first invoking the name of God. He also said he'd be spending much less time with the village imam because from now on his son would be writing all his letters.

Our city imam was now saying how "the boy must be a mine of knowledge by now." Then, turning his attention to the rest of us, he said, "But these other ones are no better than sheep. Incapable of attending school and finding food and shelter for themselves without him."

Throughout it all, the handsome boy did not breathe a word. His father, whose real destination was the capital, rose early the next morning and went off to collect whatever earnings his elder son had managed to save up. Our life went on much as before, with the handsome boy providing for us as if we were his children. We had even stopped milking the goats. The neighborhood women were keeping us in food and drink.

Then, one day, the handsome one came home in a terrible state. He took me aside and told me he had been unable to complete the letter he had been working on that day. He explained how on previous nights he would lay the groundwork, choose his words with care, select the ideas, and settle on this or that poetic flourish, but not tonight; tonight, his pen had run dry, completely out of ink.

"I'll give you ink. I'll even lend you my pen," I offered.

But it seemed that would not do the trick. "No," he said, "you must come with me. You'll write the letters. It'll be better this way. We can divide the work between us. Because frankly, this day in, day out, constant letter writing to feed the lot of you is beginning to wear me down."

"Is letter writing tiring?"

"Yes, it is. Well, I'm exhausted, at any rate. Plus, I've run out of ink. So, you'll have to take over now."

"Fine, but you'll have to teach me how to do it, and I want you to know, right off the bat, absolutely no men. I'm not writing any letter for any man. The only thing they ever want from their sons is money. And when it's not money, it's advice or insults. Now, mothers, on the other hand, write about their feelings, their hopes, and their prayers, always with plenty of love and warmth."

"You see, you know it all already."

"Maybe, but I'm going to play by Hizam's rules and protect my money and body at all times. I am not writing for any woman if her husband isn't in the room. And that goes for the men, too."

"What if a woman has no husband?"

"Then I'll ask the imam to come along. But I still can't understand why you won't borrow my pen and some ink and be done with it."

"A man must rely on his own weapons, if he is to win the battle. And I'm a man, a real one."

"Well, as I remember it, you're the only one who cried when they circumcised us."

"My point precisely. I cried because I'm a man. I felt my wound. Whereas the rest of you might as well have been sheep. Have you ever seen a sheep weep?"

"No."

"It just goes to show that you're one then. Are you sure you don't understand what pen I'm really talking about?"

"I think I'm beginning to, and I am determined to protect mine with my life, if I have to. I wouldn't want to disappoint Hizam."

"As you wish, but you'll live to regret it. I guess I'll just have to do what I can if I'm to go on putting food in your mouths."

Whenever we had a problem, we put it on the table for all to discuss, just like our elders in the village. One Friday morning, as we were sitting down to our special breakfast, I decided to bring up the handsome one's poor performance at school.

"We all did well except for you."

"You did well at what? Who do you think has been

housing and feeding you—something even your parents couldn't pull off? If any one of us has high marks to show for himself, it's me."

"But your failure at school is our failure. We want you to succeed on all fronts, and we think you can. We have lived and thrived on your generosity, but now we sorely regret it. We'd take dry bread and your success at school over all the pots of meat in the world."

"There is nothing to regret. Anyway, I've decided to move out. We're all on our own from now on."

"But we're all brothers here, and our parents are waiting for us to celebrate our homecoming."

"We'll let the village be the judge between the writer and the sheep."

"You're not planning to keep up this writing business in the village, are you?"

"Of course not. Don't worry, there is no such thing as a writer in his own land."

When the Feast of the Sheep came around and we all went home for the celebration, it did, indeed, turn out to be a feast in our honor. The handsome one brought back money and gifts of jewelry for all the women. Suddenly, his name was everywhere and on everyone's lips. He was greeted like a prince, which naturally made us sheep very jealous. We did our best to show off our report cards, but the village remained unimpressed: they had sent us off to make money, they were interested only in money, and no one gave a damn about our school reports. We faced the truth and had no choice but to stare success in the eye.

But I had true cause to celebrate. Even though his operation had not been entirely successful, Father was allowed to come home. Mother was doubly overjoyed to have both her son and her husband at home. Life, on the other hand, was changing for Sister—Father was becoming increasingly pious and had less and less time for anything but prayer, Mother was growing too frail for village work, and I was destined to wander. In the end, our father, the musician, had chosen prayers over music, and our mother, the poet, was praying from morning to night and incessantly quoting the Qur'an.

Father showed me the scar below his belly. This was the first time he wasn't hiding anything from me, and I understood that his gesture was meant to prepare me for his death. I could let go of my belief that my father's body was hewn from rock; I saw it now for what it was, flesh and bone, a body like any other, weary, a body of sun and cold, of earth and rain. His feet were smooth from his stay at the hospital, wiped clean of every trace of village life, but for how long?

We slaughtered a sheep to mark the holy day. Our sheep, as always, was one of the best in the village. Mother had fattened him up for an entire year. Father had entrusted me with the slaughtering this year, as if in this, too, he was abdicating to me. The master of the household was always the one to slaughter the sheep, with every member of his family looking on. Until now, I had simply assisted my father. And he was surprised this time when he saw me rinse my mouth with sheep's blood, as I had seen Hizam do countless times. Mother had readied the knife that was brought out once a year for this purpose. The slaughter of a sheep, or of any animal for that matter, was an art form in our village. The sacrificial gesture had to be swift, a few seconds at most, and it was sacred. This time it was doubly sacred, as our family watched the father step back and the son step up to take his place for the first time.

Mother and Sister both loved that sheep, but they also knew how proud they would feel when the time came to display it for the entire village to see. I removed my new holiday outfit and stripped down to my undergarments. Father recited the special prayer, Sister closed her eyes, and I did what I had to do. This was without a doubt the fattest sheep we, or anyone in the village, had ever seen. We strung it up in the sitting room in full view of everyone and placed a large platter under it to collect the dripping fat.

As on any holiday, the men were expected to go from house to house, but Father was not well enough and I made the rounds alone. I felt like I had lost a limb. Everywhere I went, the women first asked about Father and then about the feast, by which they meant the sheep—the sheep and the day had, over time, become synonymous. Some even inquired about my handsome friend, the writer, a subject about which I tried to remain as vague as possible. Things that happen in the city should not make their way to the village.

Later that evening, the entire family gathered at home. It was an extremely sad family reunion, because our bull had died while Father was away. I knew how news of this death must have shaken Father, this added misfortune that came to complicate his difficult operation even more.

"Look at the state of me," he said to me that night. "All my life, I've given myself to the fields. And now, I'm a wreck of a man. Don't you make the same mistake. Just keep at those books, that's where your future lies. Each to his fields. I'll see to it that you finish your studies. I'll do everything in my power, even if it means selling off my fields one by one. I don't want you to end up like me someday. I'll make any sacrifice, and you know I almost prefer to die than to part with even the measliest parcel of land."

At dawn the following morning, a self-appointed delegation turned up at our house. They sat down to coffee with Father. They had come to communicate their solemn vow to look after Father's fields until he was well enough to do so himself. The labor these men were promising was a heavy burden for the village to shoulder. Two tears fell onto my father's hands. Health, he said, is preserved by labor. No one could know his fields the way he knew them. He had spent years stroking them, singing and talking to them. All his hopes were in those fields, his strength, his youth. The life force of his entire family was in those fields, and had been since the dawn of time. He even looked after the fields of cousins who had long since left the village to strike it rich in the city.

The schoolteachers also came to pay us a visit and congratulate Father on my good grades. They took as much pride in me as he did. The serious nature of his operation had not been lost on them, and they advised him to go to the city for follow-up treatment at the hospital where the Pakistani nurses worked. As expected, Hizam was against the idea. There were, he claimed, trees right here in this village whose sap could heal anything, even heartache. Father opted for the hospital. When it was time for us to go back, he came with us and the nurses took very good care of him. He even met the neighborhood imam and paid a visit to Egypt. Our friends in the city gave him a warm welcome, especially the imam, who went out of his way to convince the local religious authorities to make Father the official muezzin at the village mosque. This meant he could be near God and get paid a salary to boot.

The imam organized a celebration in Father's honor. The two of them were becoming close as brothers. Later, they both had a talk with the handsome one. We never found out what they talked about, but shortly thereafter, the handsome one stopped writing letters altogether and was devoting fifteen minutes a day to cleaning the mosque. The imam even promised him a small salary, plus Paradise, God willing. The handsome one was extremely relieved that he had been saved by Father, and not by Hizam.

"Just think if it had been Hizam! I could've ended up with a broken pen."

"And deserved it!"

"But I had you all fooled, didn't I? Well, it's not exactly like I wasn't telling those women stories. I just kept going from one lie to the next, and I soon realized they were willing to believe anything I told them. It felt so gratifying, so pleasurable. Remember the first one, the one who would only return our belt and knife if we ate her delicious food? Well, she told me about one of her great-aunts who had lost a daughter. Later, she told me how this daughter had died in childbirth and left a child behind. Then, one day, she asked me to pay a visit to her old relative in that village we called Egypt. I soon had the old woman thinking I was her grandson. She took me in as she would a son and told me Pharaoh's secret."

"Is there any truth to this Pharaoh story?"

"Of course, there is. And this is the only story I told the women that didn't come straight from Hizam."

"Hizam? He never told you any stories."

"You're very mistaken if you think Hizam belongs only to you. It's becoming very obvious you don't know the man at all."

"Please! Don't provoke me. Here, see for yourself." I showed him the three places on my arm where Hizam had branded me with hot embers to test my virility and instill me with fire in the old ancestral way.

"Hizam never did this to anyone else, not even to his own children."

"Do you want to hear the story or not?"

"Yes, I do, but I don't want to hear that Hizam was responsible for telling lies."

"I'll tell it to you exactly as I told it to my ladies. I wrote my first letter in a house that bore the name of Egypt. I convinced the lady who owned the house, and all the women who came after her, that the vast country we know as Egypt is situated right here, in our own backyard."

"I hope you didn't attribute any of this to Hizam. Because he never much liked Egypt, and nothing galls him more than people saying that Egypt is the mother of the universe."

"Well, this house got its name for a reason. The owner is a man who comes from a small town that is also known as Egypt. Names travel like the wind, my friend. The man's last name happened to be Aoh. So, what with Egypt and Aoh, it didn't take much to think of Pharaoh. This Aoh was a sorcerer. He could heal everything, especially those illnesses that afflict women, and he believed in the properties of honey as a cure-all. He could also resuscitate the dead, or so he claimed. And the power he had over women was undeniable. Even in the dark of night they flocked to his door. Word had it that this man was as beautiful as a poem, but he never married. The other men of Egypt weren't going to put up with this for long. In the throes of jealousy, they conspired to kill him. But Aoh was onto them long before the ugly deed, and one morning he fled the village with only a sack of coffee and a jar of honey to his name. The village women named countless newborn children after him after he left those parts.

"While journeying on the Northern Road, he came upon another traveler, a man from deep south in the Peninsula, whose only luggage was a sack of flour and a bag of dates.

"'Good morning, my friend,' he said, 'I am Aoh.'

"'No, you're not. I happened to pass through Egypt just after you left, and everywhere I turned, women were crying *Phar Aoh, Phar Aoh*. I asked what all the hubbub was about and was told that *phar* in your language means to flee, and the women were crying for Aoh who had fled. So, from now on, you're Pharaoh to me. And I am Haman the miller.'

"'Fine, I'll be Pharaoh—if it makes you happy—the coffee merchant.'

"'What would you say to trading your coffee for my flour?'

"The sacks were duly exchanged. The alleged flour turned out to be a sack of ashes topped off with a thin layer of flour, and the coffee was nothing more than a bag of goat droppings covered with a smattering of coffee beans. And that's when Pharaoh uttered the famous phrase that is still used in these parts today: 'The Sorcerer of the North met his match, the Sorcerer of the South.'

"The two men became inseparable, brothers from that moment on. They hatched a plan to travel to the land of the Nile, where they heard people did not bury their dead but left them out in the elements surrounded by all the riches they had amassed in a lifetime. They journeyed far and long, and one day, they arrived in the land of the Nile, where the greenish light that enveloped both land and water was so lulling people spent most of their time sleeping and only interrupted their slumber to feed on fruits and fishes and vegetables as though they had already reached the shores of Paradise. But all was soon to change with the arrival of our two sorcerers, who poisoned the river waters and triggered a drought and famine the likes of which had never been seen.

"Pharaoh approached the grand vizier and convinced him the dead should be buried together with their loot and placed under round-the-clock watch to ensure the safety of their treasures and the eternal peace of their departed souls. The grand vizier agreed and entrusted the reform to Pharaoh. Pharaoh, in turn, enlisted Haman as his assistant.

"Pharaoh, of course, buried the bodies and kept the riches for himself. As for Haman, he was one of the richest and most powerful merchants in the city by day, and by night he assisted his old friend.

"Now, the king of Egypt had fathered only one daughter, and the grand vizier, who couldn't stomach the idea that the heir apparent was a woman who would someday perhaps even govern the country, took Haman into his confidence. Haman went straight to Pharaoh and told him how the grand vizier was onto their racket and had warned him their riches would be confiscated and the pair of them banished if the king's daughter didn't vanish without a trace in the coming week. Pharaoh came up with a plan. The princess died and was buried together with her gold with much pomp and ceremony.

"Haman and the grand vizier appeared before the disconsolate monarch to present their condolences. Seizing on the monarch's deeply afflicted state, Haman somehow managed to wrangle a private audience for his friend, the keeper of the dead. Yes, the king would see this man and hear him out. Three full days after his daughter had been laid to rest, the monarch was baffled to see Haman and Pharaoh escort her into his rooms. The king sentenced the grand vizier to death and appointed Pharaoh to the post. He also gave him his daughter's hand in marriage. Many years later, the king died and Pharaoh became king and Haman his grand vizier. And now you know how the land of the Nile got its name, from a small village called Egypt that had once been Pharaoh's home."

"What a fantastic story! I'm beginning to see why you were such a success with the women."

"I healed them with Pharaoh's remedies and always talked about you as my brother and partner, something like Pharaoh and Haman."

"Still, I didn't like playing the part of your treasurer and accountant. I couldn't help feeling ashamed, ambivalent. To me, it was dirty money, and I couldn't bring myself to talk about it, even to you. What are we going to do about it, anyway?"

"Let's go now to the place in the mountains where you hid it and we can split it. If it's dirty money, as you say, we don't have to worry because some djinn or snake will have already claimed it, and we'll never be able to get our hands on it. If it's clean, we'll find it and then we can give each woman her share back."

"Sometimes, I think you've forgotten everything they taught us in the village. If a djinn has claimed that money, then we run the very serious risk of ending up with our heads on backward. On top of which, we'll be sterile, and that's just the beginning of what could happen to us."

"Will you stop fretting? I know the money is clean. Just tell me where you hid it, and I'll go by myself."

We put on our belts and knives and slipped out of

the house unbeknownst to the rest. The secret place where I hid the money suddenly felt like a fortress guarded by invisible armies. Fear had turned my legs to lead.

The minute we reached the spot, we heard a noise that sent us scurrying up the mountaintop. From way up there on the peak, it looked as if the entire earth had disappeared. We had no idea which direction to go in or where to hide. Then, out of nowhere, I heard someone call my name. I turned to find Father in the company of the imam—they had been onto us from the start. The earth came back into view, and so did the sky. We made our way down the incline to where Father and the imam had already dug up the treasure and the piece of paper with the names of the women who had given it away. Father had already made up his mind to give the money back to its rightful owners, but the imam saw things differently. The money should go to the boy, he argued, because he made the women happy by listening to them and helped them to see things in a different way.

"This boy changed their lives forever. There's not a single one of them who will want her money back. Anyway, it's unthinkable that he should meet with them now that he has reached the age at which he can keep company only with his mother and sisters and whomever else our faith allows. If not, I'll have to answer to God for his breaches. True, that kind of thing did go on before, but now, it's different. Now, there's a Qur'an in every home. Also, there are pious people everywhere you look, even in the schools and on the radio. Today, no one can claim they don't know the rules of Islam. God protect and bless us all!"

"So, what do we do about the money?" my friend wanted to know.

"It's yours. Do with it as you wish."

"I'll keep on providing for my friends. We barely ever eat meat, you know, and we often go without soap or coffee. Whenever one of our fathers turns up, we have to rush and beg some off the neighbors. And now that you say I can't see the women anymore, we can't even count on them to help. Also, my schoolwork has suffered and I don't intend to go on cleaning the mosque for the rest of my life. There must be other boys around who need the work more than I do."

While they were going back and forth along these lines, Father apprised me of his decision to sell his silver dagger. He needed the money for a new bull. There wasn't a soul in the village, in the entire region, really, who owned a dagger of such fine quality—a *Sabb addajani,* named for the master from the country's eastern region who had crafted it. This dagger was the one thing still setting my father apart from the other village men. He always kept it in its sheath like a sword, but in fact it was far superior to a sword, because it was much easier to wear and carry. On the rare occasions Father unsheathed it for the admiration of a dear friend or a great connoisseur, it shone. Even at home we never used it, we never even touched it. I was profoundly attached to it and couldn't wait for the day when I would be allowed to wear it, not as something bequeathed, you understand, but as something borrowed. I had always known the day would come when Father would lend me this supreme token of manhood and women would look at me in an entirely different way.

When all was said and done, however, the dagger was nothing more than a symbol of prestige, whereas a bull was a vital necessity. My father liked to say that a farmer without a bull is like a flutist without lips. He decided to go see his cousin—the wealthy man who had sent me packing empty-handed when Father was ill and in the hospital. I refused to go with him. The man remained as unmoved as stone, and even had the audacity to advise Father to sell off his land.

During the month of Ramadan, there were four men who left the village and relocated to the capital, the hub of the country's religious revival. All four suffered from some ailment or other, but everyone knew they had a tendency to exaggerate their infirmities. Making the most of the generous spirit of this holy month, they spent it as beggars on the city streets. People in the capital were known far and wide for their goodness. A poet had even claimed that they had invented it. And every time these four men returned to the village from their month of begging, they were more afflicted by their souls than by their bodies.

Father tried to sell his dagger to one of these itinerant beggars. The man, unable to contemplate the idea of Father without his dagger, answered in an honest, honorable way, urging Father to estimate the cost of a bull and consider the amount a gift. Father turned down the offer.

"I could never buy your dagger," the wayfarer insisted.

"But the dagger is mine, and I'll happily sell it to you."

"You know perfectly well how I come by my money. It shames me that you should sell it, and for me to buy it with tainted money shames me even more. And I cannot let you go and share your plight with others who might take pleasure in your situation. The only thing I can do—but this is to remain between us, as God is our witness—is give you whatever you think it's worth on the one condition that it never leaves your side. This dagger was made for you, and you alone, and no one else is worthy of it, least of all me."

"I want you to have it because I want it to stay in the village."

"In point of fact, you'll be killing me with this dagger. And if I ever have the misfortune of wearing it, I'll live the rest of my life in shame. I'll never beg or shame

the village again, if that's what you want. Not that I
didn't do everything in my power to keep my face hidden and escape recognition while in the capital."

"That's hardly the issue. Now, either you buy it or
I'm selling it to someone else."

"Fine, I'll buy it."

"How much are you willing to pay?"

"Whatever you say, even though I know this dagger
has no price."

"Give me five hundred rials."

"Here's the key to my money box. Take it and help
yourself."

While the two men deliberated, the silver dagger
shone deep inside its bag of cloth. Father finally agreed
to an amount both deemed fair, and we left. Not long
after this transaction, the wayfarer disappeared from
the village for some weeks. And as long as my father was
alive, the dagger was kept hidden and out of sight.

The Sacrifice

The wear and tear of life had taken its toll on both my parents, and Sister, whom we all hoped would marry someday, helped shoulder many of Mother's daily chores. The double duty of house and field was more than Mother could handle now, and she was the one who came up with the idea of a new wife as a way for Father to retain his manhood. Yes, a bride was needed, but who? Mother suggested her best friend's daughter, but Father remained unfazed.

I was back at school in the city when a traveler from the village broke the news that Mother had left home and now lived by herself in a small house on the edge of the village. I wept, upset for my parents and for my sister, who had stayed behind with Father and now looked after two houses. I wept for poetry and music and life as I had always known it. When I came back to the village, Father was there waiting as I stepped out of the car. Our eyes didn't meet, and my kiss was halfhearted. He turned and headed toward our house, expecting me to follow. We were both locked up inside our separate pain. When he reached the front door, he entered the house alone. I had already veered onto the path that led to Mother's new house. I turned and looked over my shoulder. Father was wiping away tears and signaling for me to come back to him. Above him, on the roof terrace, I could see Sister crying.

The bag I carried on my back contained coffee, tea, sugar, and cardamom—provisions so that Mother would not lack for anything during the holiday. My eyes were brimming, my throat was dry when I reached her door. I saw my mother through my tears; she stood there like a flowering mountain, dressed in her finest clothing and smiling, more the poetess than ever before.

As soon as I stepped inside, she told me I had been wrong.

"You should have gone to your father."

"You are both father and mother to me."

"No, I'm your mother, and your home is with your father, not with me."

"I did it for you, to retaliate."

"But I'm the one who wanted to salvage your father's good standing and did everything in my power to save all the things we had worked for together, the holdings that have been in our family for generations, your father's honor. You don't need me to tell you that a house without a woman is a desert."

"You mean he didn't throw you out?"

"I left of my own volition. Your father stops by every day, your sister too. Today, we were all together for lunch."

"Then why did you leave?"

"You know full well that no woman is going to marry your father and share her house with me, and your father won't hear of divorcing me. So, I came up with this solution. I will always be your mother and your father's wife, and life will go on as it always has. I promise. Come on, let's go now and have our dinner with your father and sister."

"Let's wait until the sun sets. I don't want everyone in the village to see."

"Everyone in this village knows me and what I'm made of. It's you I'm worried about right now. What are they going to make of you and the way you behaved? They'll say you're your mother's pet. Well, I won't have it. We have to show them that even in illness and old age I can stand up for myself just as I stood up for myself when I was young and in good health."

Father greeted us by firing shots into the air. A feast awaited us inside the house. My other sisters were also there with their husbands, but the night was Mother's and she its undisputed guest of honor. In spite of the heaviness that clung to the house and the sorrow that had crept into everyone's eyes, in time I grew accustomed to the separation. Father was disconsolate. He set out every day in search of a patch of shade and spent his mornings pretending to sleep beneath a rock or a tree until I came to call him in for lunch.

Mother, meanwhile, was working on her best friend to make her come around to the idea of marrying her daughter off to Father. A friend of Father's, a builder by trade, had come to propose a marriage between Sister and his son. The man was of noble lineage, his reputation good in villages throughout the area. His son had done well for himself in the capital, better than any other boy in the entire tribe. Our family was convened to advise Father on this prospect. All approved except for one brother-in-law, who opposed the union.

"The boy and his father are beyond reproach, but there's something shady in his mother's background," he said.

"How is that?" Father wanted to know.

"As you know, the influence of the maternal uncle on his nephew can sometimes be even greater than that of the father."

"Yes? And?"

"Well, as we speak, this boy's maternal uncle happens to belong to our great tribe."

"What do you mean by 'as we speak'?"

"This uncle used to be a carpenter. And, as I'm sure you're aware, there used to be a conflict over boundaries between our tribe and the other great tribe in this area. Remember how they claimed there was a tree that marked off their land from ours and we disputed the claim because we believed our lands extended well beyond that tree, and then our tribe decided to cut down the damned tree, wipe it off the face of the earth once and for all? Well, that's when the family of this maternal uncle, all carpenters from father to son, came on board to help us, providing we allowed them to join the tribe. We didn't want a war with our neighbors, so we agreed. They waited for dark and slaughtered a pair of mature sheep. They took the fatty tails as well as fat from other parts of the sheep and wedged it between their saws and the tree, and, working through the night, they brought the tree down without a sound. When day broke, our tribe had extended its territory without shedding a single drop of blood. It had also increased its ranks by including this family in its fold, and frankly, I don't want to have a brother-in-law of such dubious lineage, regardless of his success in the capital."

Father, to his great regret, had to call the whole thing off. And only later was he gladdened, when another equally brilliant boy came asking for my sister's hand in marriage.

Mother wanted Father's new marriage to prosper. It had never been his wish to remarry, and Mother felt guilty about abandoning her companion of a lifetime at such a delicate juncture in both of their lives— lives she had filled with her patience and courage and poetry. Father, who cared and wanted to care only for her, had dismissed the wedding plans outright. He was willing to give everything up for Mother. But she refused to have their hard life's work reduced to nothing. And she knew that Father had to take a wife if Sister was ever to marry. And tradition dictated that if Sister were to marry, then I too would have to marry and take care of my parents. Luckily for me, Father did not want me to marry into the village or live the hard life he had lived. He preferred to sacrifice it all than have it come to that. No one married for personal gratification in the village, the way some rich people do these days. Marriage was a duty, a necessity that lasted a lifetime. Divorce was a rare occurrence, and usually, the women instigated it.

There is only one person I know of who never married in my family. Strangely enough, she was very beautiful and very generous. She was already old when I knew her and lived alone in a small house where I was often invited to share the delicious meals she prepared. Our visits were always conducted in absolute silence, except on the one occasion when she heard of Father's impending marriage. When I reported back to Father that the old woman had spoken, he told me she had promised she would one day. News of my father's marriage had made up her mind. She said he would have to sell off a field to pay the dowry. She knew the story of every field in the village, and she told them all to me that night. From time immemorial, marriage was the sole reason fields exchanged hands, and it was only because

of the fields that people in the village were still alive
and marrying one another.

"I already have a buyer," announced Father.

"For which ones?"

"The two small ones."

"Who is it?"

"Your brother-in-law, your Sister-Mother's husband."

"Good. They'll stay in the family."

"Yes, but they're not yours anymore."

"Well, in that case, I'm pleased to be footing the bill
for your wedding."

Father often told me that all the fields belonged to
me. He and my brother-in-law met quietly, and I never
again set foot in those two small fields. Father's marriage belonged to all of us, even to Mother. It also became the topic of conversation for the entire village,
even though other weddings were being held on the
same day. We all knew our future stepmother was
spoiled and capricious—the only daughter in a home
where her father was really his wife's wife. But he was
also the most dearly loved man in the entire village; children were especially fond of him, and all the women referred to him as God's Favored One.

Mother promised Father she would take his future
wife in hand and teach the girl everything she needed to
know. She had already settled the matter with her best
friend, the bride's mother. The two of them used to

spend hours cooking meals together, and as soon as the food was ready, her friend would send her husband off to the mosque to pray. He seemed to spend hours there, and I think that's how he got his nickname.

Father relied heavily on Mother and my sisters to help his future wife fulfill her new role in the family. Sister was already engaged, but marriage would have to wait until there was another woman to take her place in the house. Sister's wedding date had already been set for forty days after Father's.

I can't say I remember much about Father's wedding day. His new wife settled in gradually. Her mother came and spent a whole week with her to ease her into her new life. And even though she lived a mere hundred meters from our door, she slept at our house in a room that was right next to the one occupied by the newly-weds. Her husband stopped by every day to visit with his wife and daughter.

During the first week, my stepmother's behavior was impeccable. But when her mother left, she spent all her time visiting her mother's home and disappeared for hours at a time. Father was furious. He had married to have a woman at home, not to spend all his time waiting for her to come back. The situation did not bode well for Sister's marriage, and Father was deeply disappointed. Again, it was Mother who took things in hand. She moved back into the house for a few weeks.

Her best friend, seeing this move as a direct threat to her daughter, ordered the girl to stay put in her new house. To Father this was further proof of Mother's love— my new stepmother also saw it this way. We could finally devote ourselves entirely to making fabulous preparations for Sister's wedding. Somehow, I felt very sad, even though I did my best to put on a joyous front that didn't fool Sister for a minute.

All the women and girls gathered at our house on the eve of the wedding. They had come to dance, and for the last time, Mother sang while Father played and I made the rounds with the coffee tray. Tucked in my belt was the pistol I had coveted for so long. Father had finally given it to me. I was handsome to all the women that night, and I knew it.

While the other women and girls danced, my Rainbow, the girl who had often addressed me as Sky, simply sat there and looked at me. When it was her turn to dance, I saw her wipe away a tear or two; she must have been thinking of Sister, who would be leaving us on the next day and taking Mother with her to a new house. Mother, in keeping with our custom, would spend the next three days helping her daughter settle into married life. When it was time for the women to leave, I saw my Rainbow give Mother a small cloth bag that I assumed was a wedding gift.

For the three days Mother was gone, I never even

caught a glimpse of the one who never left my thoughts and whose perfume was everywhere in the house. "Your Rainbow is elsewhere," Father said without elaborating. When Mother came back, she gave me the small bag I mistakenly thought was intended for Sister. I felt as though I was holding my Rainbow in my hand. An intense joy came over me, and nothing—not poetry or rain or even life—could compare with the beauty of that moment.

And yet my parents, who had always shared my every joy and sadness, were distracted. Even their gaze seemed evasive. My-Sister-My-Memory was no longer at home. I felt a great emptiness inside. Mother asked me to open the small bag, and Father got up and left us without a word. I was happy just to hold the bag, to tie it to my belt and wear it there for an eternity without ever bothering to find out what it contained, but Mother insisted. A lock of hair and a singular perfume came tumbling out of it when I opened it.

"This is all that's yours now. The rest is gone. She is engaged to be married," Mother said.

I still remember how Mother tried to talk and reason with me, to share my pain, and how I turned a deaf ear and was dead to all feeling. We were in our house; straight ahead I could see the valley, but it all seemed dead, empty. Even the fire in the hearth was cold.

I can't remember if I went to Hizam or if he came to me at home. He had heard, but he came in smiling.

I slapped him. He held me in his arms and wouldn't let go, not even to furtively dry his own tears. Oh, my Hizam! Oh, my village! The sun was setting. I could hear Father weeping when he called us all to prayer. The village disappeared and Hizam was all I had left. He took me and we went toward the great rock we called the Memory. Against all expectations, a plant had come to life on this boulder, and Hizam never forgot to water it every evening. This was the place where women and poets came to bury their sufferings. "I saw your Rainbow here last night," Hizam said. "She came and watered the plant for me. Now, it's your turn to bury this bag and pour the water." Mother, Father, and my Rainbow's mother were all standing beside us now. Hizam placed one hand on my brow and the other on the boulder, our Boulder-Memory. I never saw the sun when it rose.

My Rainbow married, but I had left the village by then, taking my secret with me, a secret I've divulged only to the photograph of my father.

Epilogue

When I finished writing this book, I went back to the village to visit my main character, Hizam. I told him about the novel, and he asked if I would translate it for him. When I was done with the story, he only commented on how I had been reading from left to right and not from right to left as it's done in Arabic. This, Hizam concluded, meant that I had been granted an extraordinary opportunity to see things from both sides.

I thought he would be surprised to hear that a publisher had paid me money for this book, but he already knew this because I had sent all the money home to my sisters. "At least, I hope you didn't sell the village?" he asked, slightly worried. I assured him I had not. "How can anyone sell their soul?" Hizam was sorry I wasn't going to use the money to fix all the houses that were falling into disrepair, but I told him my sisters would turn the money into songs about the village. "As I don't expect to live more than a few weeks, there's something

I feel I can tell you now. I never agreed with your mother, who always saw the village as a song. But you told me once about all the women who accompanied you in your writing, and I bow my head now to all the women who saved our village." These were Hizam's words. He stood straight as a sword in front of his door and said good-bye to me for the last time.

I was correcting the proofs for my book when I heard that Hizam was in the hospital—he who acknowledged only the illness of death. The men of the tribe were at his bedside day and night. I called him, although I had a hard time imagining him on a telephone at the other end.

"Is that you, the Absentee?" the old man asked. That's what he called me ever since I left the village.

"Why did they take you to the hospital, Hizam?"

"I am almost sick," he answered, "and so is the village."

"I'll come for you, and you'll be well looked after by women who love you."

"Pakistani women?"

"No, other women, women who are much closer to us and to the village. Hizam, my book is coming out soon, and I gave it your name. But your name means 'belt' in English. The belt is the thing that reveals. The veil may hide, but the belt reveals. It reveals the poetry of women and the pride of men. It's like you, Hizam, you who never hid anything from me."

"Don't come for me, but send me the book. I will leave my knife and belt for you."

And when I received the precious heirloom, I hung it up right next to the photograph of my father.

Ahmed Abodehman is a member of the Kahtani tribe, established long ago in the Assir mountains of southern Saudi Arabia. He was born in 1949 and began to write while a student at the University of Riyadh; his poetry and journalism have appeared in a number of Saudi newspapers and literary magazines. In 1982, he settled in France, where he remains active with the daily Saudi newspaper *Al Riyadh*. Abodehman is the first writer from the Arabian Peninsula to publish in French.

Nadia Benabid grew up in Tangier, Morocco, and now lives in the United States. Her translations include Driss Chraïbi's *Muhammad: A Novel* and Zoé Valdés's *I Gave You All I Had*.